Writing Information Security Policies

Content Highlights:

Why Policies Are Important

Determining Your Policy Needs

Understanding Information Security Responsibilities

The Role of Security Management and Law Enforcement

Contingency Planning Policies

Authentication and Network Security

Internet Security Policies

World Wide Web Policies

Email Security Policies

Viruses, Worms, and Trojan Horse Policies

Encryption Policies

Software Development Policies

Writing the Acceptable Use Policy

The Organization's Responsibilities and Disclosures

Commonsense Guidelines About Speech and the Internet

Testing the Effectiveness of the Policies

Considerations When Computer Crimes Are Committed

The Policy Review Process

When the use of the Internet exploded, I found myself consulting many organizations trying to figure out how to implement security on their networks. When we started to write policies, I tried to find a reference that would help us write documents that would be effective. There were few helpful references. I wrote this book for those who want to write effective security policies but are not sure how. Each chapter is written to provide insight into the information security issues so that those involved in writing policies have a ready reference to write sound policies. When you have sound security policies in place, the job of securing the network is made easier for everyone.

—*Scott Barman*

"Policies tend to be cryptic and seen as somewhat unapproachable, especially by the technical people who really understand what they should cover. This book has an informal, practical approach with great summaries, and includes the author's real-world experiences."

Brent Deterding, *Lead Engineer/Security Services, TechGuard Security*

New Riders

www.newriders.com

Writing Information Security Policies

Contents At A Glance

Writing

Information

Security Policies

Scott Barman

New Riders

www.newriders.com

800 East 96th Street, Indianapolis, Indiana 46240

An Imprint of Pearson Education

Boston • Indianapolis • London • Munich • New York • San Francisco

Writing Information Security Policies

International Standard Book Number: 1-57870-264-X

Library of Congress Catalog Card Number: 00-105340

Printed in the United States of America

This product is printed digitally on demand.

Trademarks

Warning and Disclaimer

Publisher
David Dwyer

Associate Publisher
Stephanie Wall

Managing Editor
Kristy Knoop

Sr. Acquisitions Editor
Jeff Riley

Development Editor
Laura Loveall

Product Marketing Manager
Stephanie Layton

Publicity Manager
Susan Nixon

Project Editor
Stacia Mellinger

Copy Editor
Chrissy Andry

Senior Indexer
Cheryl Lenser

Manufacturing Coordinator
Jim Conway

Book Designer
Louisa Klucznik

Cover Designer
Brainstorm Design, Inc.

Cover Production
Aren Howell

Proofreader
Debbie Williams

Composition
Molly Sharp

❖

I dedicate this book to my wife, Elisa Joy. She was my best friend, my trusted advisor, my inspiration, and my love. She fulfilled my hope and dreams of finding happiness and love. Although cancer has taken her from this world, her love and spirit continue to live in my heart.

❖

Table of Contents

About the Author

Scott Barman is currently an information Security and Systems Architecture Analyst for The MITRE Corporation (`http://www.mitre.org`). He has been involved with information security for almost 20 years, nurturing the evolution of systems and their security requirements for commercial organizations and government agencies. Since the explosion of the Internet and prior to joining MITRE, he had focused on various areas of security and policy development for many organizations in the Washington, D.C. area. The inspiration for this book came from his SANS '99 presentation. He earned his undergraduate degree from the University of Georgia and a Masters of Information Systems Management from Carnegie Mellon University (`http://www.mism.cmu.edu`).

About the Technical Reviewers

The reviewers contributed their considerable hands-on expertise to the entire development process for *Writing Information Security Policies*. As the book was being written, these dedicated professionals reviewed all the material for technical content, organization, and flow. Their feedback was critical to ensuring that *Writing Information Security Policies* fits our reader's need for the highest-quality technical information.

David Neilan has been working in the computer/network industry for over 10 years, the last six dealing primarily with network/Internet connectivity and security. From 1991 to 1995, he worked for Intergraph, dealing with graphics systems and networking. From 1995 to 1998, he was with Digital Equipment, working with DEC firewalls and network security. From 1998 to 2000, he was with Online Business Systems, doing LAN/WAN and Internet security. David is currently running a business, Security Technologies, in the network/security realm; he is working with local companies to enable and secure their networks. He is designing network infrastructures to support secure LAN/WAN connectivity for various companies utilizing Microsoft 2000 and Cisco products and the Internet to create secure Virtual Private Networks. David also has been beta testing Microsoft operating systems since Windows For Workgroups, WFW3.11, and has worked part-time as a technical editor on many Microsoft/networking/security books.

Larry Paccone is a Principal National/Systems Security Analyst at Logicon/TASC. As both a technical lead and project manager, he has worked in the Internet and network/systems security arena for more than eight years. He has been the technical lead for several network security projects supporting a government network/systems security research and development laboratory. Prior to that, Larry worked for five years at The Analytical Sciences Corporation (TASC) as a national security analyst assessing conventional military force structures. He has an M.S. in Information Systems, an M.A. in International Relations, and a B.A. in Political Science. He also has completed eight professional certifications in network and systems security, internetworking, wide area networking, Cisco routing/switching, and Windows NT.

Acknowledgments

This book would not have been possible without the help of a lot of people. I would like to thank Al Valvano for talking to me at SANS '99 and guiding me through the proposal process. I appreciate his help in getting me started.

I would like to extend a special thank you to David Neilan, Dodge Mumford, and Larry Paccone, the Technical Editors who provided me with some very interesting comments and perspectives on my writing. Although I did not agree with every comment, I appreciated what they had to say.

Jeff Riley and Laura Loveall are two saints who put up with a lot while pushing me through this process. I know there were times Jeff wanted to hang me, and I probably drove Laura crazy, but I really appreciate your patience considering all that I had been through. Thank you!

On April 17, 2001, my wife, Elisa, died from the complications of cancer. Since her death a number of people have stepped in to provide me with emotional support to get me to this point. First, I want to thank my coworkers at The MITRE Corporation for their support during this difficult time in my life. MITRE is a first-rate organization, deserving of all the praise it receives.

To Andrea & Jaimie Rosenberg and Felice & Gabriel Bershadscky, my warmest appreciation for being special friends and allowing me to ramble when I needed to blow off steam. Hey guys, I did it!

I know my parents have been worrying about me. I can only imagine how it feels to watch their eldest in this situation. My mom, Lorri, is a special person who needs a little inspiration herself. Now that I finished my book I hope this will give her the inspiration to write hers. And regardless of what he would like you to think, my father, Marvin, is one of the biggest pussycats in the world. As much as I hate to admit it, his nudging helped, too. Thanks Pops!

I want to express my eternal love and appreciation to Elisa. She was my initial proofreader and has been the inspiration for everything that has been good in our 10 years together. She was my number one fan, and I was hers. One of my last promises to her was to finish this book. Hey Sweetiepoo, I did it!!

Tell Us What You Think

As the reader of this book, you are the most important critic and commentator. We value your opinion and want to know what we're doing right, what we could do better, what areas you'd like to see us publish in, and any other words of wisdom you're willing to pass our way.

As the Associate Publisher for New Riders Publishing, I welcome your comments. You can email or write me directly to let me know what you did or didn't like about this book—as well as what we can do to make our books stronger.

Please note that I cannot help you with technical problems related to the topic of this book and that due to the high volume of mail I receive, I might not be able to reply to every message.

When you write, please be sure to include this book's title and author as well as your name and phone or fax number. I will carefully review your comments and share them with the author and editors who worked on the book.

Email:	feedback@pearsontechgroup.com
Mail:	Associate Publisher
	800 East 96th Street
	Indianapolis, IN 46240 USA

Introduction

The growth of the Internet has inspired organizations to expand the reach of their networks. The new paradigm it fosters helps lure new customers and forge new relationships that have created a new economy that continues to defy the textbooks. The Internet also has opened electronic paths to your organization's information assets that include attackers from around the world and within your organization. The openness of the Internet magnifies need for security.

All success is the result of proper planning, especially for information security. You cannot just buy a firewall and expect it to protect your network. You need to know what you are protecting. That is what the information security policies can do. Policies are the guidelines that can be used to determine what security measures your organization should employ.

Writing successful information security policies also requires proper planning. This book helps you through the process by explaining what you need to know to write your organization's information security policies. In addition to discussing the process, it looks at different areas of security by discussing possible policy directions and offers sample policy statements to give you a greater insight.

Few references will provide the answer of what a good policy document is, and even fewer will help you write one. Although nearly every reference says that a good policy should be the basis for every successful security program, over 60 percent of companies do not have policies, or they have policies that are out of date. This book targets those who want to write effective security policies but are not sure how.

My goal is to provide a reference so that those involved in writing information security policies have a ready reference to write sound ones. In the end, having sound security policies in place should make the job of securing the network easier for everyone.

Who Should Read This Book

Security and network professionals represent a unique audience. Their job is providing front-line security enforcement while understanding the business requirements and the needs of management to keep users and customers happy. For these people, this book will provide an insight into management's policy decisions. By understanding management's perspectives, the administrator may be less likely to redefine security without consulting others.

The non-technical authors of security policies can use the book as an outline for writing effective policies. It will provide a one-stop source to understand security basics and how to address their necessity within the context of business requirements. For the technical authors, the same descriptions that will help management understand security requirements will serve as a reminder as to what they must consider. Examples of policy statements will provide insights to the formation of a solid policy.

For management, this book will provide an overview of information and network security and explain what is necessary to write sound security policies. Each chapter will discuss information security so that decision-makers can understand why they should be concerned. Sidebars and policy samples help explain trends and buzzwords that management should understand during policy development.

How This Book Is Organized

This book is organized into four parts. The following sections explain what you can expect to find in each.

Part I: Starting the Policy Process

Chapter 1, "What Information Security Policies Are," begins by introducing the idea of information security policies and why they are important. A security policy is like a project management plan, which means it omits the details of how it will be executed. Chapter 1 also discusses management's responsibility for understanding and supporting the policy and its development. Demonstrating "due diligence" is always an issue. If in the course of an "incident," inconsistencies in administration and enforcement are discovered, the lack of consistently documented and implemented policy can become the focus of the ensuing investigation.

Chapter 2, "Determining Your Policy Needs," and Chapter 3, "Information Security Responsibilities," lay the groundwork for those writing information security policies. First, Chapter 2 discusses that the writers of security policies must know what is being protected before writing policies. This chapter includes discussions of how to identify which policies are necessary for the environment. Chapter 3 defines the roles and responsibilities of the individuals in the organization for security. Emphasis is placed on the responsibilities of management and the roles of those who must provide front-line enforcement. The understanding of these groups is necessary for a successful security program. This chapter ends by discussing awareness training and support.

Part II: Writing the Security Policies

Physical security policies are easy in that everyone understands these ideas. But a good policy goes beyond the concepts of guns, guards, and gates. These policies also must consider facilities planning and disaster recovery procedures. Chapter 4, "Physical Security," outlines some policy considerations that should go into any security policy.

The basis of security is the granting of access to the system and network. Authentication is the front gate to any system or network where the user or account name grants permission to enter, and the password acts as a key to the gate. Chapter 5, "Authentication and Network Security," discusses the different aspects of authentication and system access controls along with how to construct a policy that will consider the authentication and the network architecture security tools.

If you have not noticed, Internet security is not addressed until Chapter 6, "Internet Security Policies." This is because general information security must be considered first. Also Internet security policies are difficult to write because the technology changes so quickly. Rather than create one policy, Chapter 6 discusses Internet security policies by dividing the technologies into logical groups and explaining how they influence policy development.

Chapter 7, "Email Security Policies," covers the thorny issues of email security. Various court proceedings have caused much attention to be focused on the use of email for corporate communications. Because email is the electronic equivalent of a postcard, it requires special policy considerations. From archiving to content guidelines, organizations have a lot to consider when writing email policies.

Hardly a week passes without hearing about a new virus, worm, or Trojan Horse. These problems not only cost the company money in their aftermath, but there is a loss of productivity that can never be replaced. Although these problems primarily hit one type of system, no operating system is safe. Chapter 8, "Viruses, Worms, and Trojan Horses," discusses the problem of viruses and how to construct policies to protect the network.

In Chapter 9, "Encryption," encryption takes center stage. Because transmission over the Internet is not secure, some may want to use encryption to prevent prying eyes from seeing proprietary data. Encryption has moved out of the arena of spies and the military to become necessary technology for protecting the transmission of electronic assets. From Virtual Private Networks to privacy-enhanced mail, cryptography is now in the mainstream with issues that will require unique policy considerations.

Software development methodologies have rarely considered security as a component of design. Often, security becomes an afterthought, causing unusual measures to be employed. By including software development policies, organizations can prevent ad hoc redevelopment, thus keeping their in-house development from being their security hole. Chapter 10, "Software Development Policies," discusses the software development process and how it influences organizational security.

Part III: Maintaining the Policies

The purpose of Chapter 11, "Acceptable Use Policies," is to explain why Acceptable Use Policies (AUPs) are important and how to summarize other policies for this document. The AUP is a document that summarizes the overall policy for the users. Usually, it is a signed document outlining the security responsibilities of the employee, contractor, and vendor with access to the network.

After policies have been written, who enforces them? What happens when policy is broken? Who decides how to respond to security violations? Chapter 12, "Compliance and Enforcement," discusses these and other questions that the reader should consider before executing any policy.

Security policy documents should be living documents, changing and evolving as the organization and technology changes. Policies must undergo periodic review by a team similar to that which designed the initial guidelines. Chapter 13, "The Policy Review Process," discusses the review process and provides suggestions on how to integrate this process into the company's procedures.

Part IV: Appendixes

The appendixes provide more information to help in the understanding of information security and the writing of policies. Appendix A, "Glossary," lists and defines technical terms used in the book. Appendix B, "Resources," includes additional resources for the reader who wants more information. It includes pointers to web sites that discuss security on both the general and system-specific issues. Finally, Appendix C, "Sample Policies," has sample policies to use as a guide.

Conventions

This book follows a couple typographical conventions:

- A new term is set in *italics* the first time it is introduced.
- Sample policy statements are set in *italics* and indented to highlight them from the text.

I

Starting the Policy Process

1

What Information Security Policies Are

A CLIENT CALLED ME UP ONE DAY AND asked me to come to his office. Once I arrived, he asked me to install a firewall so that his network would be secure. I asked him for his company's security policy so I could configure the firewall. He gave me a curious look and asked, "What do I need that for?"

In the years since the explosion of the Internet, this response is still the rule rather than the exception. Companies have comprehensive employee policies, sometimes filling two-inch binders, but do not have information security policies. If they do, they will hand you 5 sheets of paper that cover the assets of a multimillion-dollar corporation.

Just as employment policies describe the practices that employees and managers must take, security policies describe how the company wants to protect its information assets. That is an important concept to remember: Information is an asset. You might not be able to assign it a value, but your competitors might pay thousands or even millions of dollars to understand or even steal those assets.

About Information Security Policies

Information security policies are high-level plans that describe the goals of the procedures. Policies are not guidelines or standards, nor are they procedures or controls. Policies describe security in general terms, not specifics. They provide the blueprints for an overall security program just as a specification defines your next product.

Questions always arise when people are told that procedures are not part of policies. Procedures are implementation details. A policy is a statement of the goals to be achieved by procedures. General terms are used to describe security policies so that the policy does not get in the way of the implementation. For example, if the policy specifies a single vendor's solution for a single sign on, it will limit the company's ability to use an upgrade or new product. Although your policy documents might require the documentation of your implementation, these implementation notes should not be part of your policy.

Why Policies Are Important

Although policies do not discuss how, properly defining what is being protected assures that proper control is implemented. Policies tell you what is being protected and what restrictions should be put on those controls. Although product selection and development cycles are not discussed, policies will help guide in product selection and best practices during development. Implementing these guidelines should lead to a more secure system.

When management participates in the creation of information security policies, it demonstrates that management supports the effort, lending credibility to the entire security program. Having management support is always important. Without leadership, employees will not take policies seriously. Therefore, if you do not have the support of your upper management, your program is doomed to fail before you finish writing the policy.

How You Gain Management Support

First you can try to reason with them. You can point out that the systems and data have real costs. You can demonstrate how an outsider or a disgruntled insider can easily access sensitive information that could damage the company's business functions. You can show them studies, articles, even this book. But if this doesn't convince them, you might have to wait until your first disaster.

Management might say that everybody is responsible for his or her own security. That might work in the short term, but it prevents the company from working with itself. If one department uses one standard and another department uses another standard, interoperability could be a problem. Policies ensure that the company uses the same standards in every security instance. This consistency makes it easier for the company to integrate, interact with customers, and maintain a sense of security throughout the system.

Finally, an information security policy will help avoid liability. We live in a litigious society. If you try to enforce rules that are not expressly written, you will be sued. If you fire an employee for security violations that have never been written, presented to the employee, or previously enforced, that employee also can sue your company. I know it sounds harsh, but the reality can be devastating when the subpoena arrives.

When Policies Should Be Developed

Ideally, the best time to define your policies should be before your first security problem. By doing this early, your security administrators will understand what to protect
and what enforcement measures can be used. Also it is always easier to write policy for
a developing infrastructure rather than trying to retrofit it into an existing business
environment.

Mitigating Liability

As you might or might not know, all business processes come with a certain amount of
risk. Safeguards are placed into our business processes to mitigate this risk. A security
policy takes business processes into consideration and applies best practices to protect
them. This can help reduce the liability after loss of critical data.

As security and virus protection become an integral part of the evening news, law-
enforcement has increased efforts into catching and prosecuting perpetrators. More and
more of the courts are asked to apply our paper-based laws to the electronic frontier.
Companies without policies have found they have few liability claims because the
courts understand explicit policy and not the best practices. It is to the company's legal
advantage to have this written down before being challenged in court.

The new economy has put a premium price on electronic information. Electronic
information and the machines that store it are so integral to business processes that
companies have been looking to insure these assets. As part of a process, insurance
companies have been questioning the security policies and practices of the company.
The first question an insurance company will ask is to see your security policy.
Without a security policy, most insurance companies will not consider issuing an insurance policy. Insurance companies know that without having gone through the policy-
making process, the company does not know what assets it is protecting, therefore
making them too risky to insure.

Finally, a security policy that includes software development policies will help guide
development of more secure systems. By setting these guidelines and standards, developers can be appropriately constrained, testers can know what to look for, and administrators understand what is required during this process. Custom development always
represents a great cost and liability. By drafting and implementing software development polices and by giving developers guidelines to follow, liability can be mitigated.

After a Security Breach

Implementing policy after a security breach is like closing the barn door after the cow
has escaped. Although it might seem too late, there may be cows in the barn that you
can save. Never think that because it happened once it cannot happen again. Because it
happened once it likely will happen again.

When developing policy after a security breach, never focus on the area broken.
Although it is a concern, it is just one of many areas that should be a concern. Always

look at the whole picture—never one problem alone. This is the only way to write a comprehensive policy.

Document Compliance

Governments, government contractors, those who work for government contractors, and other businesses working in areas that involve the public sector must provide a way to ensure that their systems are safe and secure. Increasingly, governments and other customers have been demanding well-defined information security policies. Part of showing compliance is having a security policy. Even when starting new development, a security policy shows the customer that you are serious about his or her security concerns.

Government security requirements seem to change all the time. One thing that has not changed is the requirement that agencies set security policies, how the contractors follow policies, and how they work with their own policies. As more requests for proposals hit the streets, the requirements for security policies also will increase. If your company works with the government in any capacity, from contracting, to compliance, to enforcements, the presence of a security policy that can help avoid liability will be a primary concern.

Demonstrate Quality Control Processes

Along with compliance, companies also might want to demonstrate that their processes fall within quality control standards. International Standards Organization (ISO) 9001 describes a standard to demonstrate quality control in all business processes and procedures. If your company wants that type of accreditation, the policy will serve as a guideline for the implementation of a measurable security program required by quality control standards.

How Policies Should Be Developed

Before policy documents can be written, the overall goal of the policies must be determined. Is the goal to protect the company and its interactions with its customers? Or will you protect the flow of data for the system? In any case, the first step is to determine what is being protected and why it is being protected.

Policies can be written to affect hardware, software, access, people, connections, network, telecommunications, enforcement, and so on. Before you begin the writing process, determine what systems and processes are important to your company's mission. This will help you determine what and how many policies are necessary to complete your mission. After all, the goal here is to ensure that you consider all possible areas for which a policy will be required.

Define What Policies Need to Be Written

Information security policies do not have to be a single document. To make it easier, policies can be made up of many documents. Just like the organization of this book, rather than streams of statements, I divided the book up into chapters of relevant topics. So rather than trying to write one policy document, write individual documents and call them chapters of your information security policy. By doing so, they are easier to understand, easier to distribute, and easier to provide individual training with because each policy will have its own section. Smaller sections are also easier to modify and update.

How many policies should you write? I hate to answer a question with a question, but how many areas can you identify in your scope and objectives? For each system within your business scope and each subsystem within your objectives, you should define one policy document. It is all right to have a policy for email separate from one for Internet usage. It is not a problem to have a policy for anti-virus protection and a separate policy for Internet usage. A common mistake is trying to write a policy as a single document using an outline format. Unfortunately, the result is a long, unmanageable document that may never be read, let alone gain anyone's support. Figure 1.1 has sample list of policies that could be written.

Popular culture is full of examples showing that people have short attention spans. And face it, information security policies are not exciting topics. Subsequently, keeping the policies short, to the point, with clear statements, logically organized, in a cleanly designed document will give your document a better chance of being read. Do not try to overwhelm your audience.

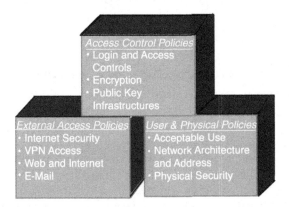

Figure 1.1 A sample list of areas that can have their own policies.

Perform a Risk Assessment/Analysis or Audit

The only way to understand your infrastructure is to perform a full risk assessment, risk analysis, or audit on the entire enterprise. By doing so, policy writers can obtain a great understanding on the reach of information technology within the organization. Although it makes the job seem ominous, it allows the authors to consider every aspect of the architecture.

As part of a risk assessment, the organization may want to do some security penetration testing. This testing should be performed both on the internal network and externally to test every known access point and to discover any unknown access points. This broad assessment provides insights necessary to understand the configuration of the network. This information should be used to determine configuration, access, and other policies. Also it will confirm how the network supports the organization's mission.

Some administrators might feel that they could explore the system, determine the risks, and inventory the enterprise themselves. Although they could possibly do an adequate job, it is always better to hire an outside company to perform this activity. The predominant reason is that they do not know your system, best practices, or other inside information that could prejudice the assessment. The outsider can come to your company and explore your systems from a hacker's point of view: Here is a potential playground, let's see where we can play! This will allow them to expose vulnerabilities, weaknesses, and other problems that you will consider when writing the policies.

Why Hire Outsiders to Do a Risk Assessment?

Some might feel that their own systems and security professionals could perform the risk assessment. I do not agree. While the people your company employs may be very competent, they are too intimate with operations to be able to tell a technical risk from a process risk. Outsiders do not have the same ties, so they cannot be prejudiced by "what has been."

When selecting an outside company to do a risk assessment, make sure they have the resources to understand the latest security information and industry best practices so that they can provide a complete risk assessment. They must understand all the risks involved in all aspects of information technology. Because these companies do this on a daily basis, they have more insights into what to expect as they perform their tests. This objective point of view will be invaluable during your policy process.

Review, Approval, and Enforcement

As with any corporate document, it is customary to have review procedures. Information security policies are different types of documents. The review process should consider not only the technical aspects of security, but also the legal aspects of it as it relates to the organization. Prior to authoring any policies, there should be a clear understanding of the overall review process. Obviously the authors will perform the first review and then different levels of corporate review should occur. If your company has a Chief Information Officer (CIO), that person should be on the review committee. Department heads or division heads that will be affected by a policy also should be able to review and provide comments. Finally, as much as everybody hates their involvement, the corporate attorneys also should be involved. Attorneys understand the ramifications of the policy in areas such as enforcement and what can be done to enforce the policy.

The approval process is a simple matter of the management agreeing to the final version of the document. Their approval should come after it is reviewed. However, if management fails to bless these documents, its effectiveness will be limited.

Finally, after the policy is written, approved, and administrators implement its directive, the policy must be enforced. Policies that are not enforced will be broken at will. It is the same as laws that are not enforced in society. Why go through the process of creating security policies if the provisions are being ignored? The policy must have provisions for enforcement, and these measures must be carried forth.

Summary

1. Security policies
   - Are distinct from guidelines and standards.
   - Are distinct from procedures and control.
   - Describe security in general terms; they do not describe how to implement.

2. Policies are important to
   - Assure proper implementation of control.
   - Guide product selection and development process.
   - Demonstrate management support.
   - Avoid Liability.
   - Achieve consistent and complete security, avoiding fragmented efforts.

3. Policies should be developed
   - Before security problems occur.
   - To avoid liability.
   - After a security breach.
   - To document compliance and demonstrate quality control processes (for example, ISO 9001).

4. Policies should be developed by
   - Setting the scope and objectives for the policy document.
   - Defining what policies need to be written.
   - Performing a risk assessment/analysis or EDP audit.
   - Defining effective review, approval, and enforcement procedures.

2

Determining Your Policy Needs

NOW THAT WE KNOW WHAT SECURITY policies are and have the support of management, the next step is to understand exactly what is being protected. This understanding goes beyond the hardware and software that makes up the system. It is very important to understand the business process that the technology supports. Your policy could sit on the shelf collecting dust if it prevents the company from doing business.

Identify What Is to Be Protected

In the first few pages of this book, I have repeated that the information security policies must protect the company's mission or business process. I did this because it is a common mistake to try to look at the computers and software from a technical point of view instead of why they were purchased. If you remember that computers are the tools for processing the company's intellectual property, the disks are for storing that property, and the networks are for allowing that information to flow through the various business processes, then you are well on your way to writing coherent, enforceable security policies.

Hardware and Software

Supporting those business processes are the hardware and software components that will be protected by the policies. Therefore, it is important to have a complete inventory of the system, which should include a map of the network. There are many ways to create this inventory or produce a network map. Regardless of what methods are used, you should make sure that *everything* is documented. Following is a sample list of hardware and software items that could appear on an inventory. This might not be a complete list for your specific environment; you should consider how to tailor this list for your company's purposes.

Sample Inventory List

Hardware	Software
▪ CPUs	▪ source programs
▪ boards	▪ object programs
▪ keyboards	▪ utilities
▪ terminals	▪ diagnostic programs
▪ workstations	▪ operating systems
▪ personal computers grams	▪ communication pro-
▪ printers	
▪ disk drives	
▪ communication lines	
▪ terminal servers	
▪ routers	
▪ diagnostic equipment	

One way to map the network is to show how the data flows through each system. A *data flow map* can show how the flow of data supports the business process as well as highlight areas where it is important to apply security and survivability measures. In turn, that map can be used to inventory where data is stored, including databases, how it travels through the system, backups, audit, and administrative logging information.

Non-Computer Resources

Inventories, like policies, must go beyond the hardware and software. There should be a list of documentation on programs, hardware, systems, local administrative processes, and other documentation that describes any aspect of the technical business process. These documents can contain information regarding how the business works and can show areas that can be attacked. Remember, the business processes can be affected by industrial espionage as well as by hackers and disgruntled employees.

Data Flow Mapping and Survivability

Survivability is the ability to determine how a system maintains its mission and critical processes in the presence of attacks, failures, and accidents. It is based on the research performed in the CERT Coordination Center at Carnegie Mellon University (www.cert.org). Their research demonstrates that instead of using the traditional fortress-like security model, networks should be considered as unbounded, independent entities with defined communications paths and specific trust relationships.

Analyzing a system for survivability involves understanding the business requirements of the network, the architecture of the network, how it is used to satisfy those requirements, and a trade-off analysis to ensure the survivability measures also maintain the business environment. Part of the analysis and the usage requirements is the understanding of how data flows through the system. By understanding this flow, an analysis of critical processes can illustrate where resistance should be applied and demonstrates necessary limits placed on the architecture by the business requirements.

For more information on CERT's survivability research, see Appendix B, "Resources."

Similarly, the inventory should include all pre-printed forms, paper with the organization's letterhead, and other material with the organization's name used in an "official" manner. Using blank invoices and letterhead paper allows someone to impersonate a company official and use the information to steal money or even to discredit the organization. So, include those supplies in the inventory so that policies can be written to protect them as assets.

Taking Inventory of Human Resources

The most important and expensive of all resources are the human resources that operate and maintain the items inventoried. To inventory the people involved with the operations *and* usage of the systems, data, and non-computer resources will provide an insight as to what policies are necessary.

Creating an inventory of people can be as simple as a typical organizational chart of the company. This can be cumbersome, however, if you are including a thousand or even a few hundred people in one, big document. Moreover, organization charts are notoriously rigid and do not assume change or growth. The inventory, then, could include the type of job performed by a *department*, along with the level of those employees' access to the enterprise's data. For example, if the company has a large sales department, creating an organization chart with everyone's name may serve the egos of those included, but the chart becomes unmanageable. Rather, the inventory can include the "Sales Department" noting that some number, which may be unspecified, of salespeople work there.

One positive aspect of this exercise is that management can gain an understanding of who is working for the organization and in what area. As part of this process, management can see duplication in processes, identify strengths and weaknesses, and show where there might be organizational problems. This type of analysis is similar to survivability of network systems—but on a human scale. Managers should not have to be reminded to act appropriately during this process.

Identify From Whom It Is Being Protected

Defining access is an exercise in understanding how each system and network component is accessed. Your network might have a system to support network-based authentication and another supporting intranet-like services, but are all the systems accessed like this? How is data accessed among systems? By understanding how information resources are accessed, you should be able to identify on whom your policies should concentrate. Some considerations for data access are

- Authorized and unauthorized access to resources and/or information
- Unintended and/or unauthorized disclosure of information
- Outline enforcement procedures
- Bugs and user errors

Primarily, the focus will be on who can access resources and under what conditions. For example, human resource data can be accessed by authorized human resource personnel but not by the general user population. The policy might need to allow direct access of personal data but should define what "direct access" means. Of course, the policy would limit access to those who should not have this type of access as well.

After you define who can have access, a consideration needs to be made as to what enforcement mechanisms and penalties should be placed on unauthorized access. Will the organization work with law enforcement? What disciplinary action will be placed on employees who violate the policy? Legally, what can be done?

Legality of the organization's actions is very important. In this litigious society, it is important to specifically state the ramifications of violating the policy. In some states, it may be enough for the policy to say that the employee can be dismissed and "prosecuted to the fullest extent of the law." However, others may require specific language explaining the applicable laws. This is where having a lawyer on the policy-writing committee can be helpful.

This advice extends to access of the organization's systems through external means. By saying "external means" we are not limiting access to just the Internet. Access can come through Virtual Private Networks (VPNs), private networks (such as a customer network that uses Frame Relay), or modems. These access points must be defined, and policies must be created for what can and cannot be accessed from them. Because access policies are a very important basic protection to any organization, the topic will be covered fully in Chapter 5, "Authentication and Network Security."

As the software development cycle gets condensed to work within what has been called "Internet time," we all must live with bugs and user errors. These are unintentional intrusions on the secure operations of a network that can interrupt mission-critical operations. Although it is difficult to anticipate what to do in the case of failure or errors, it should be included as part of the analysis. One way to think about how to consider non-intentional problems as well as possible intrusions on the systems is to use Survivable Network Analysis Method (SNA) for analyzing network survivability. See Appendix B for pointers to the papers on the SNA Method.

Survivable Network Analysis Method

When analyzing the network for survivability using the SNA method, the first three steps are to gather the system definition, understand essential capabilities, and assess compromisable capabilities before performing the survivability analysis. These steps are essential for the analyst to understand the nature of the mission for which these systems work—thus understanding and allowing for necessary tradeoffs in design that can be important to the analysis. Using SNA, the architecture and usage scenarios are used to analyze how the network is used.

The key to SNA is that it requires the definition of two types of network usage scenarios:

1. Normal usage scenarios (NUS)

2. Intrusion usage scenarios (IUS)

NUS analysis defines how the system and components should be used under "normal" conditions. Thus anything that is not normal can be considered for intrusion analysis. IUS can be defined to understand the potential impact of a successful attack or accident. This type of analysis is very useful to understanding how the network components inter-operate.

Data Security Considerations

Everything we do with computers and networks allows the flow and usage of data. Every company, organization, and government agency is focused on the collection and use of data, regardless of their function. Even manufacturers have critical data-handling aspects of their operations that include pricing, shop floor automation, and inventory controls. The handling of the data is so important that in defining the policy needs and collecting inventories, understanding the use and structure of the data (as well as where it is stored) should be a requirement of all involved with writing security policies.

Handling of Data

How will data be handled? There are many aspects of dealing with data that must be considered when writing policies. The policies must consider how data will be handled and how to maintain the integrity and confidentiality of the data. In addition to the handling, consideration must be made to how handling that data will be audited. Remember, data is the lifeblood of your organization; you should have mechanisms to trace its life through the system.

What about using third-party data that may be confidential and proprietary? Most data sources have associated usage and auditing agreements that are included with the acquisition of that data. As part of the inventory of the organization's data, external services and other sources should be added to the inventory. The inventory also should identify who works with the data and under what conditions this data is collected and possibly disseminated.

Care and Handling of External Data

External data can be defined as any information collected, bought, or given by a source outside the company. Many times this data comes with copyright or confidentiality agreements that dictate how the information is used. Whether it is information or the source to a vendor's latest release, mechanisms must be in place to enforce the agreements by which that data is acquired and used.

One trap is the collection of information from public data sources that are incorporated into other works. It is easy for employees to cut-and-paste information from web sites and other sources into internal documents. While this is legal under fair-use standards, the employee should provide proper attribution, especially if the information is quoted verbatim. Yes, they should know better. However, this should be reinforced by the policy and be included in the security awareness program.

Just as other organizations share information with you, you also might want to share information with them. Whether it is because of a partnership agreement or other business relationships, mechanisms must be in place to protect the disseminated data or technology transfers as intellectual property. When writing these policies, some of the considerations for disseminating intellectual property are

- Use of company information for non-business purposes
- Definition of intellectual property-handling requirements
- Transfer of information to a third party:
  1. Confidentiality agreements
  2. Full-disclosure records
- Protection of disclosed data

It is difficult to anticipate how the business circumstances define what can be disclosed and how, but the policy should include a review of these processes. One way to understand their impact on policy is to understand how current agreements are handled. As part of the inventory process, any attorneys working on the committee can gather these agreements and notes on current discussions. Using this information, policies can be written as guidelines to protect the company in information and technology transfers.

A common omission to these policies is the requirement to classify information. One common method is the use of security labels. Although the use of security labels is not consistent across all operating systems, databases, and software programs, policy writers should consider how to mark data for their level of security. There are many circumstances where this is necessary. In particular, personnel or health care information are prime candidates for security labeling.

Personal and Personnel Data

During the course of business, an organization can collect personal and personnel information in many ways. Those involved in e-commerce may collect information from access to their web site. Companies that sell products and services can collect customer data through order/entry or customer service calls. Even sales calls or potential customer inquiries can yield personal information about a person or a company. Regardless of how this data is acquired, policy statements should be created for everyone to understand how the data is used.

Privacy Polices and Public Policy in the United States

As I write this, public policy makers in Washington are discussing the practice of collection and handling of personal data during the normal business cycle. In recent news, the Federal Trade Commission (FTC) has recommended that congress pass laws requiring companies to disclose how they handle information they collect from access to web sites. This came after finding that many web sites do not have posted privacy policies or policies that are followed.

Currently, the FTC privacy guidelines are merely guidelines and not part of public law. At the FTC's request, Congress is looking into the issue. As with many controversial issues, predicting what Congress will do can be a full-time job.

One thing to consider when beginning this process is how your organization operates outside your home country. U.S. companies doing business in Europe, for example, might be subject to strict privacy laws in Germany and Scandinavia. Although these policies may not be popular within your organization, it will help when working outside the United States. For further information, see Appendix B.

When considering privacy policies, the observance of privacy must be defined so that the organization not only observes the employee's or customer's right to privacy, but also that the employee observes the organization's right to privacy. Policies can be written to state that private, proprietary, and other similar information should not be disclosed without prior consent.

Privacy policies are not easy to define. Because policies are guidelines and not procedures, some organizations prefer to define exactly what is protected in procedures documents. One of the best ways to determine how to partition this is to gather what should be included in privacy policies and look for one or a short number of common statements. Those statements become the policy. How the data is handled then becomes a matter of procedure.

COTS Licensing

Policies for Commercial Off-The-Shelf (COTS) software licensing must consider that in most cases, the organization does not own the software or the data governed by those licenses. COTS licenses allow you to use the software under specific restrictions. This means that COTS policies should be based on following those licenses.

The software industry has been increasing their licensing enforcement procedures through the Business Software Alliance (BSA) industry consortium. Working from tips that usually come from disgruntled employees, the BSA audits and reports on the licensing status to the owner of the software. After an investigation, the BSA supports the company in filing breach of contract lawsuits against offending companies.

Strong COTS policies should include the periodic review of licensing agreements, guidelines for acquisition and evidence of software licenses, and records of registration of products with vendors. Additionally, policies on copying should be included and should mandate strict management and accountability of those resources.

I have heard one common theme when discussing COTS policies with others: Software licenses are assets and should be treated as such. This is not a far-fetched idea. These licenses are tangible assets that have value, can be counted, and can be depreciated like the machinery on the shop floor. This will please the Chief Financial Official if he or she has not considered the value of software to determine the amount spent on property, plant, and materials.

Backups, Archival Storage, and Disposal of Data

Policies about the handling of data backed up to external sites or off-site media is as important as for online accessible information. Backup data can contain financial information, a history of customer interaction, and even copies of current business. If the data is not to be kept, what would happen if the competition were able to obtain and analyze that information? What if they found data that should have been discarded? Backup policies, therefore, must reflect on the processes themselves, cover how the data is archived, and provide direction for what to do when data is to be discarded.

Backup Considerations

Why does your organization back up information from its computers? Is it to recover from system crashes? Preserve critical data? Does your organization want to keep a snapshot of system software? How often are these backups made? Are they made daily, weekly, or monthly? And how do you do them? How often is this process reviewed and verified?

All good questions, but how do the *answers* to these questions enable the backups to support the recovery-critical business processes after a failure? An inventory of the business process also should include the recovery processes and the information processing that is necessary to support them. That knowledge will help determine how to answer those questions and set policy.

A common mistake in setting backup policies is to mandate the special options available in the software package the company is using. When determining how backups support the business process, policy writers should try to confine the document to describe what should be done and avoid mandating special options. The following are a few questions to be considered when analyzing backup policies:

- Which data will be backed up?
  - Only user data?
  - The whole system?
  - Entire database or journal files?

- How often should backups be made?
- How are backups to be performed: automated, multiple copies, or media?
- How often are the backup procedures reviewed?
- Will you use off-site or on-site storage for backup media? How will you secure the on-site storage area?
- Who will be allowed to perform the backups?
    - Who will be allowed to have access to the restorable data?
    - Who will be allowed to restore that data?

Archival Storage of Backups

For some, the last consideration of handling backups is how to store the media or safeguard the data. As part of the audit and inventory of operations, special note should be made of current practice. If the current practice does not safeguard data, then here is your chance to make the safeguards policy.

When considering backup archiving, one of the first concerns might be whether the media will be stored on-site or off-site. Some organizations have storage vaults for storing tapes and disks. For them, policies for on-site storage should be sufficient. Otherwise, understanding the current and best practices can help create a workable policy.

Several years ago, I retrieved a tape from the vault where my company stored its backup tapes. The vault was climate controlled and specially designed to store up to 6 years of 9-track tapes. The tape I chose was created only 18 months earlier. I mounted the tape on the local drive and tried to read its contents. After spinning for only a few hundred feet, the driver printed an error and the system refused to read the tape.

After trying several tapes, I looked at the service log and found that the system's field engineer adjusted the drive heads after someone complained about not being able to read a tape sent by a client. Although the adjustment was necessary, tapes for the three months prior to the repair date were unreadable. Had we known this would be a problem, there would have been a chance to recover the data. Unfortunately, there was not a policy on handling the data or checking the backup. Since then, I have insisted on a clause to include testing the archive.

That brings me to another point: Why was the vault nearly filled with six years of archives? Did we need six years of data? We did, but does the data that your organization stores require it to be saved for that long? If not, then how long? In cases where the retention time is longer than the life of the media (the typical life of magnetic tape can last an average of two years), maybe you should consider a policy that specifies *write-once media*. Notice that I said "write-once media." Remember the lesson learned in Chapter 1, "What Information Security Policies Are": By considering a policy with general wording, you allow the people creating the archives to determine the best technology to use. This allows for the use of new technologies that may allow the data to be archived longer than current options.

Disposing of Data

"Dumpster diving" is a common practice when those practicing industrial espionage seek information on their target. A colleague who used to work in this area would surprise me with stories about what some companies throw out. One day, he hit the jackpot. He collected more than two dozen cartridge tapes from the dumpster of a competitor that contained information that the company should have made sure was kept confidential.

How does your organization dispose of data? If you are throwing away tapes without erasing them, then the dumpster divers will surely find your company's secrets. Determining how the data is disposed of is as important as determining what data to discard. Make sure that this policy specifies how to erase or discard the data *and* that it defines a requirement for verifying that the data can no longer be read.

One way to ensure that this policy will be carried out is to assign the responsibility to discard the data to one person and the verification to another. The policy should mandate that a regular schedule or a rigid procedure be followed so that both responsible parties can verify that those who should not see it could not access the data.

Intellectual Property Rights and Policies

Every organization, regardless of its function, has intellectual property that it protects from disclosure. Even if the organization does not have information security policies, it probably has rules and procedures for safeguarding its intellectual property. Not every organization puts the same emphasis on this property, however. For example, a company that is a price differentiator will guard its manufacturing process to prevent its competitors from discovering how they can keep their prices down.

Intellectual property policies are probably the most difficult for most information security professionals to write. Not only are these policies tied to the business process, but the body of law covering intellectual property covers volumes and can differ between states and countries. When planning and writing these policies, it is highly advisable to consult an attorney whose specialty is in this area. In the preliminary stages of planning, the following are a *few* considerations for intellectual property policies:

- *Who owns the rights to the intellectual property?* Assignment of patent, copyright and other intellectual properly rights should be stated in a policy, whether it is within the information security, corporate, or employee manuals. Having this spelled out in a coherent policy can provide a solid basis to protect the company's property in court if that should become necessary.

- *What are the rights to programs and documentation?* After ownership of the intellectual property has been established, what rights do employees have with the programs, processes, and documentation? While an employee might have access to the manual that describes the latest business process or the new re-engineering plans, the policy may prevent them from taking that manual out of the plant or talking about that information with others. And the policies can define who those "others" are. In fact, some policies require that procedures define access rights to the document and processes:

- *All sources of information should have an attribution.* Graphical User Interfaces (GUIs) and the World Wide Web make it easy to gather then construct information by copying from the browser window into the window running the editor or word-processing program. Sometimes it is too easy. Making copies of someone else's work and incorporating it into your own without attribution is plagiarism. Yes, you can use small sections under the "fair use" laws, but these sections must be attributed to the original author. The policy statement can say that the company will not tolerate plagiarism while leaving attribution standards to style guidelines.

- *Labeling for paternity rights to intellectual property.* If the work is covered under patents, copyrights, or nondisclosure, it must be labeled with the appropriate information. Without quoting the cases, several have gone against the owners of intellectual property when they did not make their rights known nor took measures to protect those rights. Some companies mandate that all printed material contain the words "Company Confidential" on all pages. Labels must be conspicuous and clearly state ownership. Your attorney who specializes in intellectual property law can help in this area.

When working with intellectual property, whether it belongs to your organization or you acquired it from someone else, make sure you know your rights under the agreement. For example, many software programs allow the user to create one copy for backup purposes but not allow more than one copy to be running at any given time. As for written works, there are still "fair use" laws that allow a limited number of copies for personal use. Once the usage is allotted for business purposes, you should talk with your attorney about what is and is not allowed.

Technical People and Intellectual Property

There are many urban legends regarding the handling and protection of intellectual property. One of my favorites says that a way to copyright a work without filing the necessary papers is to mail ten copies to yourself. The postmark on the unopened envelopes would be enough to establish the date and location of the work.

Technical people tend to work hard on an idea, and then they take these legends seriously in an attempt to save money. Later, they find that these schemes offer no protection. Intellectual property is such a complex subject that myths and legends should not be your guide in protecting your organization's most important asset. Instead, talk with an attorney who specializes in this area. The attorney will tell you that all you've done with those ten envelopes is added money to the coffers of the postal service.

Incident Response and Forensics

I think I subscribe to every information security mailing list. These lists give me varying levels of details on the bugs and other vulnerabilities that can cause security problems within systems or networks. Some are general while others are run by manufacturers and cater to users of that vendor's product. Most contain information submitted by users while the rest comes from the manufacturer. I know that the number of mailing lists I am on is overkill to most administrators, but the point is that as I work with my clients, I am kept up to date on the latest information.

Yet one day, you are sitting in your cubicle, and you discover a security hole that once publicized, if attacked by a hacker or a disgruntled employee, could bring down the organization's network. Rather than trying to bury the information, you try to publicize it.

Some people feel that incident reporting is an important service to the Internet community. So they go out of their way to report problems they found. Many of these organizations have a policy for incident reporting. You can send the information to over 30 different incident response organizations. To help these services, your organization could have a policy to work with one (or a few) incident response team(s) through one point of contact. By limiting the responsibility to one person, or a backup, information can be efficiently transmitted from a single, authoritative source, and it will not be lost in a sea of messages that might even conflict.

The CERT Coordination Center

The granddaddy of all the incident response teams is the CERT Coordination Center (CERT/CC) at Carnegie Mellon University in Pittsburgh. Founded as the Computer Emergency Response Team in cooperation with the Department of Defense following the Internet Worm in 1988, CERT/CC collects information about security incidents and investigates whether or not it is a problem that should be publicly disseminated. Although CERT/CC's methods are considered controversial, they do provide a valuable service to the community. CERT/CC is not the only incident reporting service. Appendix B provides a list of a few others.

Incident Response Strategies

On the other end of incident handling is incident response. Incident response is necessary when unauthorized access of your network is detected; when a response team contacts your organization to say that problems exist, and that they appear to be coming for your organization's computers; or when someone reports to a public service that a problem was found in the operating system or support software that your organization runs.

Like incident reporting, incident response policies should have one point of contact. That person should be responsible for collecting these reports and preparing a response to them, regardless of from whom they come. In fact, the contact person should be able to determine if an incident report is applicable to the organization. The policy could give this person the power to do whatever is necessary to solve any problems arising from these reports or provide the ability to draw on others necessary to diagnose the problem.

Working with vendor-supported response teams is similar to working with independent services, except the vendor may contractually require your organization to choose a particular point of contact. For example, your organization might want the security officer to handle incident responses. Your vendor might want to bypass this person to work with system administrators. Allowing this requires only a minor adjustment in policy and can be written in a way to allow for working with vendor teams.

Computer Crime

As I write this, I am looking at three different guidelines for prosecuting people under different attempts at defining what is a computer crime. Each guideline tries to tie the local jurisdiction's case law (the decision and opinions made by the courts) to the written law. The only consistent theme is the inconsistency of their requirements.

Understanding what is a computer crime differs between jurisdictions. Even in the United States, each of the federal court circuits may have different interpretations of the same law. If you are a company in New York, the rules may not be applied the same to your office in Silicon Valley. The key to understanding what is allowed in your area is to make an appointment to speak with the district attorney, attorney general, or solicitor that you would work with. They know the judges and the standards of evidence necessary to successfully try a case.

However, writing a policy saying that the company will work and report all criminal activity may not be in the company's best interest. Take the story of the bank whose systems were infiltrated by hackers who stole nearly $11 million! That bank initially chose not to report the incident to any law enforcement authority fearing negative publicity. With billions of dollars in assets, it was easy to write off $11 million in "lost" funds.

One day, the bank had to report the loss in response to another lawsuit. When the press found out about how this bank lost $11 million, the negative publicity was enough to affect the price of their stock and garner additional scrutiny from federal regulators. The end result was a public relations problem, which costs.

Determining what to report and under what considerations is not something to take lightly. Policies in this area must be discussed among executive management, who must bear the burden of the decision should something happen. On the other hand, requesting that management make the decision about the appropriate policy forces them to consider security policies. How they answer will tell you how seriously they are taking these efforts. At this stage of policy writing, it is good to know how much support really exists.

Summary

This chapter discussed the need to understand exactly what is being protected. This understanding goes beyond the hardware and software that makes up the system but integrates the business process into the preparation process. Your ability to support your policy decisions will determine the success of the document.

1. Identify what is to be protected:

    - *Hardware.* CPUs, boards, keyboards, terminals, workstations, personal computers, printers, disk drives, communication lines, terminal servers, and routers.

    - *Software.* Source programs, object programs, utilities, diagnostic programs, operating systems, and communication programs.

    - *Data.* During execution, stored online, archived offline, backups, audit logs, databases, or in transit over communication media.

    - *Documentation.* On programs, hardware, systems, and local administrative procedures.

    - *Supplies.* Paper, forms, ribbons, and magnetic media.

2. Identify from whom it is being protected:

    - Unauthorized access to resources and/or information

    - Unintended and/or unauthorized disclosure of information

    - Bugs and user errors

3. Data security considerations:

    - Handling of data (integrity and confidentiality)

    - Handling of third-party confidential and proprietary information (who's allowed and under what conditions)

    - Protection of disclosed data (confidentiality agreements and full-disclosure records)

    - Personal and personnel data (rights to privacy and disclosure policies)

    - COTS licensing policies (periodic review, registration, evidence of compliance, and copying)

4. Backups, archival storage, and disposal of data:

    - *Backups.* What, when, how, how often, and how often reviewed.

    - *Archival storage of backups.* On-site storage versus off-site, protection of archive, documentation, testing, retention period.

    - *Disposal of data.* Who is responsible and how it is verified.

5. Intellectual property policies:

    - Information as an important company asset

    - Assignment of patent, copyright, and other intellectual property rights

- Attribution of sources for information
- Labeling for paternity rights to intellectual property
- Protection of intellectual property rights (notices and due diligence)

6. Incident response and forensics:
   - Incident reporting and response strategies
   - Determining who has this responsibility
   - Working with industry and vendor response teams

7. Computer crime:
   - Understanding that a computer crime really is only considered such according to law enforcement
   - Determining what to report and under what considerations
   - Working with law enforcement

3

Information Security Responsibilities

I F YOU ARE READING THIS BOOK IN chapter order, you probably want to start writing the policies. However, before you start to write your policy documents, you should really have a clear definition of the roles and responsibilities of the individuals in the organization with respect to security. As we have discussed in the first two chapters, management support is crucial for a successful information security program. Along with its support should come responsibility to the ongoing maintenance of this program. This chapter will emphasize the responsibilities of management and the roles of those who must provide front-line enforcement. The understanding of these groups is necessary for a successful security program. The chapter ends by discussing awareness training and support.

Management Responsibility

Management's responsibility goes beyond the basics of support. It is not enough just to bless the information security program; management must own up to the program by becoming a part of the process. Becoming part of the process is showing leadership in the same manner as it does in other aspects of the organization.

When I tell this to people in management, I get a reaction of shock or horror. After all, they are not trained in technology or information security. I explain that they do not have to understand how it works, but they need to be involved to ensure that the business processes are protected and not hindered by security decisions. Management has specific goals for the organization, and most security and information system professionals are not in the position to understand or appreciate these nuances. This is not a knock against management or technical people, but years of misunderstandings have created animosity between the two groups.

Both groups should understand that security is not something that can be wrapped in a package and bought off the shelf. It is a goal that both parties strive to maintain. It comes after the analysis of risks, costs, and the requirements to ensure that information is not too secure to access. Management is responsible for doing the analysis and conveying this to the technical people responsible for implementing these policies.

Information Security Management Committee

One of the ways to help bridge the divide between the two groups is to create an *Information Security Management Committee*. This committee will be responsible for reviewing changes in the business plan and determining how the security policies should support those changes. Another purpose of this committee could be to review the procedures, assuring that they comply with the policies as well as requests for exemptions to the policy.

To make this committee a success, it should be made up of a diverse population and be similar in makeup to the group that authored the policy document. However, the difference is that this committee should consist exclusively of management representatives who will understand the implication of the policy from both the business and technical perspectives. This assumes that technical management understands the issues and has access to information to help make good decisions on security issues. Not every member needs to be executive-level management, but it would be a good idea for the committee to be represented by someone from the executive suite.

Information Ownership

One of the more difficult tasks for management, or even the management committee, is to assign responsibility for information assets or controls—also called *information ownership*. By designating an owner, that person becomes responsible for maintaining the information asset according to policy.

Information ownership is not an easy concept for many people. In the traditional security model, data and controls are kept on the servers under the watchful eye of an administrator or administrators. That administrator, then, must understand how that system is used and how to set access controls. Problems occur when the administrator has to manage a diverse set of controls for many different servers, databases, data stores, or just "assets." To keep a sense of order, the administrator makes policy implementation decisions based on the least common denominator of everyone those systems serve.

In this "one-size-fits-all" scenario, the administrator sets the classification, sensitivity, and access controls for the data to be consistent with the assessment of his or her job. There is no guarantee that these attributes will be compatible with the policy as it applies to every person that accesses the information. Conflicts can occur between users requiring access to information and administrators who have made the wrong assumptions.

An alternative method would be to assign ownership of the data and controls. The owner would be responsible for defining access to the data and determining how the controls are to be set. The owner would work with a security and/or systems administrator to manage the information assets. The owner would determine the sensitivity and classification instead of leaving it up to the administrator. This result would be the managing of assets to satisfy the needs of the owner.

The owner would be responsible for handling variances from generally accepted practices. If the request for information requires controls that are inconsistent with policy, the owner is then responsible for the necessary changes and subsequent repercussions. Some organizations require information owners to request variances in writing and sign a disclaimer taking full responsibility for any potential problems. Because many do not want to take the career risk involved with this responsibility, requests for variances are rare.

The downside to information ownership is that the owner is responsible for maintaining controls in a manner consistent with the security policy. Further, some owners may feel that the requirement to take full responsibility is not fair or not worth the risk, thus they do not follow procedures and ignore policy. From the beginning, the owner must understand the impact of the responsibility he or she has to the information. The only way to mitigate this problem is through proper security awareness training, support from management, and consistent and stringent enforcement.

Another problem with information ownership is that it only really works well in diverse organizations where data can be partitioned among potential owners. I have not seen this work well in marketing organizations or in others where data is thoroughly integrated in the environment. Information ownership also can be a problem in smaller organizations where there may not be enough people to support this concept. One company I worked with that tried information ownership made all 20 employees co-owners of the data. Although this was done as a morale booster, it also helped maintain the integrity of the data.

If your organization is not comfortable with the concept of information ownership, you might want to adjust your policies to create committees of responsibility. By creating small committees, they can do the same thing owners would do, but no single person would have to accept responsibility. Rather, the entire committee becomes the responsible party. This creates a situation with additional checks and balances when variances are requested.

Assigning Information Ownership

The first rule of assigning information ownership is to make stakeholders the owner of their own data. Simply, the owner of financial data should be someone under the Chief Financial Officer. This is not an easy process. The point is not to create catch-all departments, unless it fits the business process. This also means that the Information Systems Department must not be the owner of information except that which is needed for operations such as configuration, user identification information, domain name service (DNS), and the like.

As part of the process, you should talk to the stakeholders. By discussing information ownership with those directly involved, you can understand their concerns. You might even get ideas regarding how to assign or structure ownership.

Ownership should be assigned based on a high-level inventory of information assets. You can use the same inventory as created during the preliminary processes (described in Chapter 1, "What Information Security Policies Are"). I suggest the high-level list be used so that there are not too many information owners. It may require additional analysis into who should own what information, but limiting it to a few key players will help manage the process. Then, each major information type should have a designated custodian assigned from the inventory.

Security Responsibilities for Information Ownership

If your organization decides to assign information ownership, you have to consider what responsibilities these owners have. Guidelines written into the policy should define the specific controls information owners are allowed. By "specific," I mean what controls they can work with, not how those controls are implemented. These policy statements also can discuss the administration of the access controls in terms of the parameters they are allowed to administer.

The most important responsibility given the information owner is the granting and revoking of access to the company's information. As you begin to draft policies, those dealing with the access of information should include how these policies affect the information owner. Further, access policies also should consider recovery capabilities for the data and the access control processes. For example, the policy can mandate that

- If the information owner is not available, the owner should designate someone to act on his or her behalf.
- Passwords used in management of the information are also held in a password or key escrow so that they can be accessed should something happen to the owner.
- There are mechanisms to override the information owner.

Remember, the mechanisms you are considering are policies. Avoid the temptation to define the procedures information owners will follow.

Information Security Compliance Plans

When discussing management's responsibility and compliance, you should concentrate on how management should respond to enforcement as well as when policies are broken. These plans go beyond the issue of management support. These discussions should center on the roles management should play in the information security arena.

When it comes time for awareness training, management's sessions are exclusive and abbreviated compared to what everyone else must go through. Rather than separate management, see if you can integrate management into the security plan. Make management an active participant. While it is not necessary to have an executive actively review log files or site-inspect facilities (although they might be a good ideas), they should be involved with settling disputes and counseling employees that violate policy. Should a problem require the assistance of law enforcement, members of management should be on hand as an active participant in the investigation.

This may be tough to sell to nontechnical management. Even in the move to automate business processes, management that does not understand technology tends to hide behind their technical people or consultants. Although information security is not really a technical issue, it is seen as such. One way to include them in the process is to have them own the processes, just as other managers own the data. By making them the owners of the processes, it will give them a sense of responsibility, which will not allow them to wilt behind their desks and management committees. For that sector of management whose ego needs a boost, giving them responsibility will add to it.

Role of the Information Security Department

The Information Security Department is responsible for implementing and maintaining organization-wide information security policies, standards, guidelines, and procedures. They should provide security awareness education and ensure that everyone knows his or her role in maintaining security. Simply, the Information Security Department provides the mechanisms that support the security program outlined by the policy.

This department must be able to strike a balance between education and enforcement (see the "Security Awareness Education" section that follows). It will be difficult to find this balance. The policies guiding this group should be written down to ensure that these roles are clearly defined. They should be viewed as a partner in the business process. If implemented as an enforcement-only group, the Information Security Department will be feared. Fear can elicit adverse reactions to its real purpose, which can undermine the purpose of these policies.

Chapter 12, "Compliance and Enforcement," as its name makes obvious, is dedicated to compliance and enforcement, an integral component of security awareness education. Read ahead if you need more information about the role of training before continuing with the policy-writing process.

Security Awareness Education

The importance of security awareness training and education cannot be overstated. By taking the policy seriously and teaching all of the stakeholders about their role in maintaining it, they will embrace the policy as an integral part of their jobs. This is not easy. One problem is that over the last decade, industry-leading companies have not demonstrated a concern for security in their products. The results are products that have insufficient security measures installed into environments that further weaken the information security program. The dichotomy can be confusing.

Security awareness training requires clear communication. One thing you might consider for your organization is hiring a technically competent communicator for the Security Department. This person would do the training, educate the department to the concerns of its users, and act as a liaison between users and the department. Having someone who can communicate will help raise the confidence level users should have for the department.

Use of Consultants for Information Security

Outsourcing has been a staple of the computing industry since companies offered time-sharing services on expensive mainframe systems. Today's outsourcing environment can provide information processing services for every aspect of the organization, including information security.

There are some serious concerns in using consultants or outsourced services for information security. When determining policy goals for the outsourced environment, a few things should be considered:

- *Work with in-house Information Security Department.* It is highly recommended, even if information security is outsourced or consultants are used, that the organization maintain a small department—even if it consists of only one security expert. Information security is something that requires a trust relationship among the users of the information and those enforcing the policy. It may be difficult for some to trust an outside source.

- *Set clear guidelines.* As with any outsourcing or contractor agreements, clear guidelines on the roles and responsibilities must be defined for these outsiders. It may not be in the organization's best interest to provide these outsiders open access to the information assets. Therefore, a clear *statement of work (SOW)* should be included as part of every outsource information security agreement that clearly outlines guidelines. The SOW should not be part of the policy documents, but its guidelines should be stated.

- *Determining responsibility.* Another aspect of the SOW should be to determine the responsibility of the outsourcing or contractor in the organization's information security environment. Policy should include the responsibility of anyone working as part of this environment.

Other Information Security Roles

For any information security program to be successful, it must be integrated into every aspect of the environment. Integration must include statement of work and responsibilities within the business environment, job descriptions, and how these will be audited and monitored.

Integrating Information Security into the Business Process

A primary task in assigning roles in the information security process is how information security integrates into the business environment. As part of that integration, jobs that support security through the processes should be defined. For example, one way to do this is to define a separation of duties and control over company assets by coordinating efforts with everyone, including owners of data and facilities. By having these defined as part of the business process, there is no ambiguity as to who is responsible and when.

Another role to consider is how security is administered throughout the organization. A typical environment should have a central information security management group. The central group is in charge of the monitoring and enforcement of the policy and procedures. Consider an approach from unbounded systems (see the description in Chapter 2, "Determining Your Policy Needs") where the central security management group designates security administrators for multi-user and multi-departmental systems. Each department then supplies its own security officer or liaison who will help maintain the security program for the department. This has the effect of putting enforcement closer to the users, sort of like police departments returning to the concept of the cop walking the beat.

The closer placement of security enforcement will help with the control of real-time connections with third parties. Not only do threats exist from employees, but customers, vendors, and anyone else with connection to the organization's information assets can violate policy. These liaisons can be responsible for educating these outsiders as well as monitoring and providing enforcement. This works in smaller organizations. Many compartmentalize themselves into "departments" that can participate by assigning one person as a security liaison, especially when working with people outside the organization.

This, however, is not a perfect solution. Some people who work in this environment for an extended period might find ways to abuse the system and exploit it, for whatever reason. One way to combat this is not to allow a person to be the security liaison for more than a short period of time, one or two years for example. At the end of the term, they pass the job to someone else. Another way is to set a policy of checks and balances. One manageable process is the organization's procurement system. Even though most purchases have an approval process, many times those approvals are passed along and paid without further notice. Instead, a security liaison within the Accounting Department should look for anomalies in purchases and orders shipped.

Those who do forensic accounting tell me it is not an easy job and is a job that cannot be done by just anyone. The forensic accountant must know the business process, customers, vendors, new business, old business, and how the money flows through the organizational machine. Using this knowledge, the forensic accountant can read invoices or purchase orders and determine if there are unusual purchases or sales that may indicate an internal problem.

The final area that should have a role in the information security process is the software development cycle. Whether software is developed internally or by contractors or if the organization purchases Commercial Off-The-Shelf (COTS) products, the goal should be to build secure systems wherein errors or manipulations can be trapped. Policy for coding and testing standards also can assist in the quality assurance process. Moreover, using a paradigm such as survivability (as described in Chapter 2) can form a basis for designing software that does not cause or reveal problems when deployed.

Individual Information Security Roles

One way to ensure that every current and future employee or user knows that security is part of his or her job function is to make it part of each job description. Spelling out the security function or expectations within the job description demonstrates the commitment to information security as well as emphasizes that it is part of the job. After it is made part of the job description, it becomes something that can be considered in performance evaluations.

Outside contractors, vendors, or other people that provide external services directly on the company's network should include similar language within their SOWs. As with employees, this reinforces the company's commitment as well as makes the contractors' or vendors' adherence to the organization's security requirements a factor in their quality-of-service evaluations.

Auditing and Monitoring

Auditing and monitoring are important for enforcement and compliance of security. However, if this is not a role within the business process, there is a danger that it may never be done. Think of this process as the quality control of your information security program. That way, the roles required to provide internal audit of information system controls will be a natural occurrence and not considered a surprise attack.

In later chapters, we will talk about the independent review process. For now, however, consider it a role of someone to arrange and supervise this review.

Understanding Security Management and Law Enforcement

As I write this, it is being reported that Microsoft was allegedly hacked by overseas intruders. News reports are saying that the hackers supposedly used viruses to plant

Trojan Horse programs, hackers were able to download Microsoft's proprietary source code. There have been other famous intrusions and manhunts for the perpetrators. Unfortunately, with the exception of a few high profile cases, most of the electronic trespassers do not get caught.

Compared to other areas of law enforcement, computer crime and information forensics are in their infancy. Like in the days of the Old West, the police today must face the problems that arise from any new experience. First, there are jurisdictional concerns. The nature of the Internet, multi-national corporations, and the growth in worldwide telecommuting blurs the borders between states, provinces, countries, and continents. If they ever find the perpetrators of the Microsoft break-in and that person is from overseas, under whose laws will they be prosecuted?

Whose Jurisdiction Was It?

In 1999, computer students in the Philippines wrote a virus that attacked a popular commercial mail program that caused millions of dollars in estimated damages from the cleanup. When the experts traced the messages to the Philippines, the U.S. Justice Department worked with Philippine officials to have the hackers arrested. Justice Department officials claimed that they had jurisdiction over the alleged crimes even though the perpetrators were Philippine citizens on home soil. Philippine officials could not arrest them because there were no laws covering their alleged charges.

The United States does have an extradition treaty with the Philippines, but how effective is it to bring these hackers to the United States to stand trial? Thus far, the hackers have been charged with misdemeanors and are still in the Philippines. It will take a long time for diplomats to understand the impact of computer crime and the treaties that are necessary to protect national and international infrastructures.

Another problem is understanding how computers impact the law. Although there are a number of laws covering computer crime, they are still written to conform to a paper-based world. Even though there are examples of how the laws covered the telephone as it evolved, legislators have yet to learn from those experiences, leaving us with a variety of laws.

I am telling you this not to discourage you from working with law enforcement when a crime is committed. On the contrary, I want to prepare you for what will seem like an uphill battle to bring an alleged criminal to justice. The first thing you can do is to know the law. I understand that administrators and security people are not trained in the law, but there are many resources that can help you understand what kind of protections the law provides (references can be found in Appendix B, "Resources").

Another important aspect of the law is understanding what is required to prosecute crimes in your jurisdiction. Not only are the laws different across borders, but in the United States, applications of federal laws differ between the districts of the U.S. Courts. Unfortunately, the federal district courts are like fiefdoms; precedents in one do not affect another until ruled on by the Supreme Court. This means you have to understand what the rules are for the district where your case will be handled.

One of the best ways to understand what it will take is to ask your local law enforcement officials. It is very common for physical security professionals to discuss their plans with police and prosecutors. However, with the exception of the FBI through the National Infrastructure Protection Center (NIPC), you may not get cooperation because they may not understand how to help.

Do We Need an NIPC?

The National Infrastructure Protection Center was formed in 1998 by a presidential directive to serve as a resource from which law enforcement could gain knowledge on how to protect the growing critical information infrastructures. Although it is a noble concept, there are some who believe that the FBI should not collect and keep this information. Some have even harked back to the days of J. Edgar Hoover keeping files on alleged subversives. Should the FBI be involved with collecting this data?

Although it has stumbled a bit, the NIPC has provided a lot of good information to law enforcement. The NIPC's InfraGuard program is designed to bridge the public and private sector to protect information resources. Its success will depend on the cooperation it receives from industry. To learn more about the NIPC, visit its web site at www.nipc.gov.

The primary area of focus after a crime has been committed is the handling of evidence. As part of your preplanning, learn the rules of evidence. The rules of evidence are the guidelines prosecutors must follow to legally use evidence in court. Use the guidelines to outline policy for handling data, systems, networks, and log files after a crime has occurred. Expand this into clear procedures to accompany the policy to make sure evidence is properly protected. After all, without evidence a prosecutor can use, there can be no case, and the criminals remain free.

Information Security Awareness Training and Support

After the policies are written, there must be communication among the writers, management, and everyone in the organization so that all understand the policies and impact. In this final step of the planning process, the planning for training should be considered. It is reasonable to mandate that training be required for anyone with access to company computers and networks. Human Resources should have complete records, including information on training courses required and taken as well as all signed documents showing acceptance of defined corporate policies.

Management should not only set aside time for training; they should *encourage* it. One company I was involved with mandated training during specific time periods; and unless employees were involved with a client or ill, they were required to attend. The policy allowed the employee to be suspended without pay until he or she attended the course or watched it on videotape. You might not want to go to this extreme, but it is a good way to get 100-percent compliance.

Remember, you are writing many policies and customizing them to your environment. This means that you cannot plan on a "one-size-fits-all" training program. Plan on customizing training as it relates to the contents of the policy. Also understand that everyone does not have to be trained in all areas of the policy—Help Desk personnel, for example, do not need to be trained in software development security policies. As you plan your training policies and programs, keep this in mind to ensure that each aspect is properly covered.

Summary

Management support is crucial for a successful information security program. Along with its support is a responsibility to the ongoing maintenance of this program. We emphasize the responsibilities of management and the roles of those who must provide enforcement. To have a successful security program, these groups must have a good understanding of their function and be willing to take action. The level of compliance measures this success. Compliance can only happen if everyone knows about the policies through a comprehensive training and awareness program.

1. Management responsibility:
   - Participate and support an Information Security Management Committee.
   - Information ownership includes assignment of responsibility for information asset controls; someone is the designated owner, and the owner determines sensitivity and classification, including handling variances from generally accepted practices.
   - Devise information security compliance plans for management.

2. Role of the Information Security Department:
   - Policies should state that the Information Security Department is responsible for establishing and maintaining organization-wide information security policies, standards, guidelines, and procedures.
   - This department is responsible for education, enforcement, and protection.
   - In outsourcing or use of consultants for information security, set guidelines determining responsibility to work with the in-house Information Security Department.

3. Other information security roles:
   - Regarding the integration of information security into the business process, define the separation of duties and control over company assets, coordinating efforts with everyone, including owners of data and facilities.

Designate a security administrator for all multi-user systems while specifying that each department should have an information security liaison.

- Determine the security responsibilities for real-time connection with third parties.
- Make provision for a forensic review of invoices for abnormal purchases or sales.

- Place information security responsibilities in job descriptions and in third-party contracts, and consider them in performance evaluations of both.
- Regarding auditing and monitoring, the internal audit of information systems controls is a key role integrated into the business process.

4. Information ownership and custodial responsibilities:

- In assigning information ownership, the Information Systems Department must not be the owner of information except that which is needed for operations. Ownership should be made using a high-level inventory of information assets. There should be at least one designated custodian required for all major information types.
- As part of the security responsibilities of information ownership, define allowed controls and how those controls will be administered. These controls should have guidelines for granting and revoking access to the company's information and provide recovery capabilities.

5. Understanding security management and law enforcement:

- Understand and know the law and the rules within your jurisdiction.
- Understand the rules of evidence and how to ensure that the evidence is admissible in court.
- Preplan the company's responses with law enforcement and prosecutors to understand how to handle data and conduct an investigation after a crime has been committed.

6. Information security awareness training and support:w

- Training must be required for all workers with access to company computers and networks. Human Resources should have signed forms saying it is required and another verifying the courses taken by each employee.
- Management must allow time for training and should encourage it.
- Training must be customized to the contents of the policy.

II

Writing the Security Policies

4

Physical Security

THE FIRST THREE CHAPTERS DISCUSSED THE preparation required to write information security policies. In this chapter, we begin to look at policies for physical security. Physical security policies are easy because everyone understands the idea of physically protecting property. But a good policy goes beyond the typical concepts of guns, guards, and gates. These policies also must consider facilities planning and disaster recovery procedures. This chapter outlines some policy considerations that should go into any security policy.

Computer Location and Facility Construction

Twenty years ago, preparing a location for computers meant finding a corner of the basement, installing raised floors panels, enhanced power, an air conditioner, and running cables through the walls and ceilings. It was very common to see wires piled up in offices. Converted janitor closets were used to house communication connectors. Computer rooms were cramped, out of the way, and poorly designed. A lock was put on the door so that only authorized personnel could enter. In essence, the computer systems were treated like idols where the worshipers of information came to pay homage.

During the editing of this chapter, I was reminded also of the environmental dangers caused by poor choices in placement of computer rooms and wiring closets. I was told by one of my editors that he had a job where the network operations center was six feet from the water main. Another problem was that air conditioning for that room was separate from the rest of the building, and the intake vent was next to the exhaust for the emergency diesel generators. My editor reported that someone almost died of carbon monoxide poisoning because he did not want to leave his post. The point is that in addition to attack scenarios, physical security must take into consideration any issue that would affect the operations of the systems or network.

The PC revolution and the growth of network systems changed the landscape. Facilities were being built with cables built into the walls, leaving only outlets facing the office. Network equipment was installed in specially designed rooms or "closets," and servers were given their own centers within the office. While this was a good development, not a lot of care was taken in choosing the location of computer *centers*. Their placement within buildings was a function of convenience rather than security.

Many people will read this section and say that it should be simple, common sense. I agree with that assessment. Unfortunately, I have seen several cases where critical information systems were installed in rooms with glass walls, rooms with a single source of power, and insufficient locks or barriers, making the organization's critical information systems susceptible to a physical attack and mishap.

Facility Construction

The best secure physical installations can occur when the organization builds a new facility or moves into one that can be customized. The organization can design wiring closets, server rooms, and optimal wiring for communications and expansion, making operating the information facilities easier. Even if your organization is not as fortunate, there could be a policy on the construction of these facilities.

Policies governing facility construction should be kept simple and general. First, look at the current facility. Where are the computers, servers, and communications equipment located? Define it in nonspecific words. For example, consider the policy statement of a company running a mainframe system within a major city. Its computer is located on the 10th floor with multiple secured entry doors to a room with raised floors, high ceilings, fluorescent lights, and two fire exits. This company could have a policy that reads

> *Computing facilities shall be of sufficient size and be located on any floor other than the ground floor, with multiple entry doors and more than one fire exit.*

Notice that the statement ignores the raised floors, high ceilings, and the lighting. These items, though important, can be called implementation details and should not be specified. Thus, if raised flooring is no longer required or a new type of light works better, you will not have to change the policy.

The Language of Policy Documents

The language used to write policy documents is as important as that used to write this book.

Language, specifically the style of language used to make policy statements, can say as much about the document as it can about how the organization views the policy.

It also can send the wrong message. If the language is too formal or too wordy, the rank and file could think that the policy "talks down" to them. If the language is too informal, they might not take the policy seriously. The key is to strike the right balance.

Throughout this book I give samples of policy statements using a simple but formal style. The statements are written without using buzzwords or slang. The real formality comes with my tendency to use the words "shall" or "shall not" in policy statements. Those who work with the federal government will recognize it as being similar to a style that they might see in a request for proposal (RFP) or statement of work (SOW).

Interestingly, the statement mandates the size of the room without giving specifics. By saying "the facilities shall be of sufficient size," the policy is mandating that those designing computing facilities define sufficient. Subtly, enforcing this policy provision will ensure that the computing facilities are seriously considered during the design of new office spaces.

One thing to consider with facility construction policy is the availability of redundant power supplies or access to public utilities. Redundant power supplies can mean anything from the electric company supplying the facility with power from different power grids to an uninterruptible power supply (UPS) that will supply the computer with battery power and give the administrator time to shut down the systems and everything in between. The difficulty comes with writing a policy that includes electrical requirements. The policy must reflect physical and economical realities as well as consider what is necessary to protect the business process. For example, a bank might require full redundancy for systems that run the automatic teller machines but a limited backup for the systems that support their tellers during business hours. A policy statement could read

> Computing facilities shall be located on a floor capable of solid construction with multiple entry doors, fire exits, and that allows for access to redundant power supplies.

Locks and Barriers

When I talk to organizations about something as simple as doors and locks, I get strange looks after they stop laughing. On many occasions, doors, locks, and other barriers are not considered in facility construction. However, if you are going to create a policy to ensure that the information assets are in secured rooms, remember to say something about the doors and other barriers. Improper doors can be a weak link to your physical security program. So, consider what it would take to have doors or other barriers that are impenetrable to forcible attack.

As you look at these issues, understand that doors play a role that goes beyond access control. Fire resistant doors and barriers can prevent or reduce damage. Fires outside the room can be kept out while fires within the room can be kept in and possibly extinguished before spreading. These doors should be sealed, and you should even consider self-closing doors so that they remain efficient fire barriers. Policy for these types of doors should not only talk about their use but also include a statement that says that these doors should not be propped open.

Environmental Support

I was helping an organization with their policy and asked what they wanted to say about environmental support and controls. The lead manager looked at me and asked what they needed beyond air conditioning. I looked around their room and saw large, antistatic rugs near the servers and started to ask about the environment of the room.

Every aspect of the environment is open to having a policy. Understanding what it takes to control static, maintain proper humidity (the main contributor to the static problem), temperature, and air quality can make the difference between ignorance of problems and mitigating them. The policy statement could read simply

> *The areas used for the servers shall have sufficient environment controls that include temperature and humidity controls to protect against static electricity.*

Power conditioning, the conversion of electricity so that smooth, even currents are available to all information system components, is not necessarily an environmental concern. However, given that we are looking at maintaining an environment and that electricity requirements are really an implementation detail and not a policy concern, power maintenance can be included in this section.

Inventory Maintenance

Do you know what is supposed to be in the server room? Does that phone line belong in that communications closet? *Inventory maintenance* is keeping track of what your organization has and where it is supposed to be installed. Knowing your organization's equipment inventory can prevent someone from installing a rogue computer or communications device in your facility.

Inventory maintenance policy can mandate that equipment be tracked and identified. Identification marking can be equipment tags with metal or another tamper-proof material. It is even reasonable to mandate that the equipment tags be readable by electronic equipment, either bar codes or embedded electronic inventory tags similar to those used to prevent shoplifting in department stores. These technologies can be used with computer-assisted equipment tracking hardware and software to assure an accurate inventory of information assets.

Facilities Access Controls

Putting up walls and barriers can help keep people out, but who is allowed in? Policies maintaining access controls as well as records of who has accessed information facilities can be used to complement construction policies. If you do not understand how these policy areas complement each other, try writing facility access policies before writing facility construction policies.

Building Access Controls

Having worked for companies of all sizes, including government contractors, I have seen a number of different measures used to restrict access to buildings, computer rooms, and equipment closets. Most use a system based on an identification badge with the user's picture and some coding as to their clearance or status within the organization that helps set their access permissions. In most cases, these badges have magnetic strips or other electronically readable cards.

For smaller organizations, this type of access control may not be necessary. However, that does not mean that something is not required. After all, you do not want just anyone to be able to enter your site and cause damage. Remember, access controls are put in place to ensure that those who should not have access cannot enter these areas. It is not a good idea to ignore these policies, regardless of the size of your organization.

Regardless of the policy, the organization needs to maintain records of who has access to the organization's facilities. This should include admission to the offices where someone can have access to computers used by the rank and file as well as the support facilities, like cable and communications equipment. Physical access to the communications equipment will allow someone to install taps or other eavesdropping equipment. Once an outsider has this type of access, the entire network is compromised.

Access Policies and Industrial Espionage

Industrial espionage happens daily. Whether it is between large corporations, dot-com start-ups, or government spying, industrial espionage is an attempt by one company (or country) to steal another's information assets. There are a lot of ways to steal information. One method is to gain access to the network and servers where the information is stored. The idea behind access control policies is to keep away those involved in espionage by letting enforcement personnel know who is allowed access.

Auditing access control records, including records of who has accessed secured areas, may be a requirement. In fact, this is a common requirement for those working on secured projects for the federal government. Regardless of the reason, a clear policy to maintain these records should be included within access control policies, as follows:

> *Facilities access controls shall be maintained through an automated identification process that includes procedures to add and remove people from databases or lists that control access to the company's facilities. These procedures must be auditable.*

> *Further, records shall be kept as to who is allowed to access each area of the facility and logs maintained that can identify everyone who has entered and exited each secured area.*

Notice that in this sample policy statement, no technology or procedure has been specified. In fact, it leaves open how the procedures can be implemented. If your organization uses its Human Resources Department to manage access controls, a statement can be added to give them the responsibility:

> *…from being allowed to access the facilities. Procedures for access controls shall be managed by the Human Resource Department…*

What to do when a worker is terminated is as important as maintaining access control. Of course you want to restrict his or her access, but to what degree? Some companies may allow leaving employees to have access to their offices to remove personal items. Others will require escorts and, in the case of those in areas requiring government security clearances, armed guards may be necessary. Regardless of your organization's situation, policies should address these access situations. Remember, your Human Resources Department could consider this their domain, so you should work with them to ensure that an acceptable policy statement makes it into your document.

Restricting Access to Computer Facilities

When discussing overall access controls with systems managers, they are overwhelmingly unwilling to give up the control over physical access to "their" systems. This type of ownership resolve is laudable (see Chapter 2, "Determining Your Policy Needs"), but sometimes it can get in the way. System managers can be an integral part of the process, but it might be better to have another process.

Setting physical security policy for computer and communications systems requires the same care as for the facilities. However, because these systems are managed differently from the overall facilities it is reasonable to have separate policies for these areas.

When considering physical policies for computing facilities, there are three major areas to think about:

1. The type of overall access to computing facilities. It is reasonable to call the computer center a "closed shop," which will make general access "off limits."

2. Determine access to storage areas where magnetic tapes, extra disks, and sensitive documentation is stored.

3. Consider the computer and server rooms to be sensitive business areas and restrict access to visitors. Unlike the times when companies wanted people to marvel at their mainframe systems, computers and servers are now ubiquitous. By keeping unknown people out of the server rooms, you restrict visual access to potential configuration weaknesses.

Even if your machine room contains spinning tape drives processing megabytes of data daily, it is more important to protect those central assets than to put them on display or to let just anyone have physical access.

Visitors

Regardless of the organization, there will be times that visitors will be on-site. Whether the visitor is around for meetings or are service personnel, there should be policies that guide visitor procedures. Common among these policies is to require positive identification and a sign-in record. The sign-in could require that the visitor observe company rules and regulations by remaining with an escort.

When writing a book that tries to cover a broad audience, I have to remember that not every organization has hundreds of employees and contracts with the federal government and can require many of these policies prior to awarding contracts. However, setting prudent visitor policies is a good idea for any organization. It is not a good idea to allow visitors to have free reign over their movements within your organization's facilities. It might even be a good idea to include a statement requiring employees to confront anyone without proper credentials.

Having policies that govern visitors is an attempt to prevent potential vulnerability for industrial espionage. Understand that it is possible for a visitor to do anything in the name of gaining an edge in competition. This is true for a small company as well as a government agency. An example policy statement for visitors follows:

> *Visitors shall be required to provide positive identification before entering any company facility. Once allowed inside, the employee shall escort the visitor during their time on premises.*

Contingency Planning

When terrorists bombed the World Trade Center in New York City in 1993, hundreds of companies were shut down during the evacuation of the buildings known as the Twin Towers. The closing of these buildings resulted in the loss of billions of dollars in revenue. Within three months, almost half of the companies had gone out of business. Most of the survivors had contingency plans that allowed them or subsidiaries to continue with business while the building remained closed. If you want to discuss the importance of contingency planning, ask the workers of those hundreds of companies who found themselves without jobs because their companies went bankrupt.

Emergency Response Plans

Nobody wants to think about what could happen if his or her office building were bombed, consumed by fire, or devastated by some act of nature. But it can happen, and you are better off being prepared to respond. Although it is beyond the scope of a policy document to define the plan, a policy can set guidelines for creating a plan. These guidelines can discuss handling of data, how to leave the systems, and have a provision for ensuring the saving of life and limb over information systems. One possible policy could read

> *The System Manager shall maintain an emergency and disaster response plan that will discuss what will happen in the event of a disaster to organizational facilities. This plan shall ensure the integrity of data and the ability to quickly recover when the disaster has passed. Any plan created from this policy shall include provisions to preserve life and prevent bodily injury by creating multiple scenarios and allowing employees to choose not to participate when they are in eminent danger.*

Disaster Recovery

The preceding policy statement says that the System Manager will maintain the emergency plan. It does not matter who maintains the plan or if your organization uses a committee approach, but there should be some statement on planning and maintenance of the plans. The goal of the policy statement is to ensure a maintainable (viable or actionable) plan is created. Like all procedures, there should be some provision for periodic audit and update. The following can be added to this policy statement:

> *This disaster recovery plan shall undergo a periodic review in a reasonable time frame with a minimum duration between reviews of one year. The review and audit procedure shall include a plan to test the procedure.*

Security Alert and Alarms

Part of contingency planning is to have an alert system in place that will notify the appropriate people of disruptions to monitored systems. Policies covering alert and alarms should include notifying management. Management, in turn, should be responsible for keeping everyone informed of disruptions or foreseen outages.

One thing to consider in these policies is to recommend that contact information be kept available. If your organization is a 24/7/365 operation, the policy may include provisions for an on-call system where key personnel are available during nonworking hours.

General Computer Systems Security

The intent of policies covering the general security of computer systems is to make provisions that keep the systems running and available to the business process. Thus, factors such as maintenance and outages (planned and unplanned) become the focus in this section.

Preventative Maintenance

A fundamental denial of service, especially in large systems, is unavailability because of a failure that could have been prevented. Some people have told me that preventative maintenance is a common-sense operating procedure, but I have seen companies neglect this aspect of their infrastructure. By not having a policy requiring preventative maintenance, your organization can run the risk of allowing fundamental problems to bring down the entire business process. Even if you believe it is an operations problem, you may want to mandate it as a security policy to ensure that it gets done.

System Availability

There will come a point when outages are necessary. In general, policies covering the ability to create downtime or making selected services unavailable should be controlled and limited to procedures involving a few decision-makers. These policies should limit the user's abilities to delay or interrupt services and establish mechanisms to override the normal allocation of resources for critical business functions, also called *control overrides*.

Control overrides fall into both the physical and operational policy categories. Because they require manual intervention, I like to keep them with physical system availability policies for consistency. Understand that overuse of control overrides could mean that resources are not being properly used for the organization's mission. Given that control overrides are exceptions, I like polices that try to limit their use because of the potential for denial of services. One example can read

> Procedures shall be established to allow a limited use of controlled overrides of system resources. These procedures shall establish a path of ownership of the decisions for the controlled overrides that can be logged and reviewed.

Periodic System and Network Configuration Audits

One day, an Internet watchdog group told a System Manager that one of her systems was sending out a lot of unsolicited email. After she investigated, she found a system, installed by a key employee, was being used to send those emails from within the company. Nobody knew that this system was installed in the server room, and there was no record of the server belonging to a project. After further investigation, she found that the server was installed two years earlier, and it even had its own registered domain name.

To prevent something like this from happening again, the manager started to perform quarterly configuration audits. Yes, the company had a configuration management plan, but it did not include audits to check for the installation of rogue hardware. Because this manager was overseeing a diverse and dynamic shop, she felt a quarterly configuration audit was a good idea and had it added to the company's security policy.

However, if your company does not add a lot of hardware or make significant changes, your policy may specify longer periods of time. It is recommended that this time not be longer than one year. This will give us a policy that could read

> *The Operations Manager shall conduct a system and network configuration audit at least once every calendar year. The Operations Manager may conduct audits at other times when deemed necessary.*

Notice that the policy statement also specifies a system audit without defining what a system audit is. Depending on the type of systems being used for the organization, this type of audit can take on a number of meanings. It is difficult to be specific in a policy document. If the policy is changed to mandate having an approved plan, what to include in an audit can be discussed as an implementation detail:

> *The Systems Manager shall author a plan to audit the system and network configuration. This plan shall include procedures for auditing the hardware configuration, connectivity of the network, and installed systems components. The plan shall be approved by a committee consisting of the Systems Manager (and other department heads). This committee shall review these procedures annually or as needed. The audits shall be conducted at least once every calendar year. The Systems Manager may conduct audits at other times when deemed necessary.*

Although not included in this policy statement, it might be a good idea to have someone audit the system who is not involved in its configuration. This way, you limit the possibilities of the auditor covering up his or her own security violation.

Staffing Considerations

Policies about staffing direct how the human resources are handled when managing the infrastructures. This includes policies mandating the maintenance of an inventory of key technical jobs and cross-training of personnel. This does not include policies on hiring, performing background checks, and interview procedures. These usually fall under domain of human resource policies. Remember this when your Human Resources Department objects to having this included in an information security policy document. A compromise would be to have this policy under both domains.

Before government employees and government contractors write me nasty letters, this is a broad generalization based on my experience with helping companies write security policies. Government (civilian or military) and government contractors may be required to have policies about their hiring practices and obtaining security clearances. Even though they might be requirements for working with and for the federal government, these policies are usually part of the organization's Human Resources Department.

Summary

Physical security policies go beyond the typical concepts of guns, guards, and gates. These policies also must consider facilities planning, management, and disaster recovery procedures. In this chapter, we discussed how to look at policies to physically secure the organization's infrastructure.

1. Computer location and facility construction:

   - Facility construction policies should consider the location of a new computer or communications center and where the facility is located within a building. These policies may consider how facilities can access redundant supplies or public utilities resources.

   - Locks and barriers policies should not only consider what it takes to maintain physical security from human intervention, but nonhuman causes such as fire. These policies may address the requirement and maintenance for self-closing openings as well as the treatment of windows.

   - Environmental support policies cover treatment for static electricity and other physical environmental factors, such as air conditioning. Environmental policies can include power conditioning to servers and other information assets.

   - Inventory maintenance policies are concerned with the tracking of information assets by marking information system equipment with identification codes that could even be used with computer-assisted equipment tracking.

2. Facilities access controls:

   - Building access controls goes beyond setting access policies but should discuss who maintains the access list and that it should be auditable.

   - Restricting access to computer facilities defines the policies for physical security measures for computer and communications systems. Consider making the computer and server areas "closed shops" and restricting access to backup media and documentation libraries. These measures also may prohibit public tours of computer facilities.

   - Policies for visitor access controls can include requirements for identification and sign-in processes, escorts, and required third-party supervision in areas containing sensitive information. Throughout the facility, if badges are required, individuals without identification badges must be confronted.

3. Contingency planning:

   - Policies specifying emergency response plans should specify the goals of the plan and state that the priority is the safety of the employee.

   - Disaster recovery policies should cover planning and maintenance of contingency plans including provisions for periodic audit and update.

- Management should be notified when security alert and alarms are activated. Policies should remind management to notify appropriate personnel on disruptions and foreseen outages. This policy area should consider specifying off-hours contacts.

4. General computer systems security:

   - Preventative maintenance procedures should be established to ensure continued operations of the critical information resources.

   - Assure system availability by limiting the ability of users to delay or interrupt services and by the establishment of policies for control overrides.

5. A policy to perform periodic system and network configuration audits can be used to prevent rogue hardware and software from becoming security risks to the organization.

6. Staffing policies usually concern themselves with an inventory of key technical jobs and the cross-training of personnel. Other policies about hiring and security clearances are usually left to Human Resources.

5

Authentication and Network Security

NETWORK SECURITY ENCOMPASSES NOT ONLY securing the Internet, but securing every network connection and interface. How permissive these interfaces are depends on requirements, their function, and the trust that exists on both sides of the connection. Policies securing the network and interconnects are part of a network security program that covers issues such as network addressing, subnets, and how to manage network connections.

Trust relationships are established through a narrow definition of what interconnects are allowed to pass. Regarding access to the information resources, the basis of access control is the granting of access to the system and network. Authentication is used to grant that access. This chapter discusses how to construct a policy that will consider the architecture of a network as a security tool. We will discuss the different aspects of authentication and network access controls along with what needs to be considered for securing remote access points.

Network Addressing and Architecture

A concept that is difficult for some to understand is how a network's architecture and addressing schemes can be used in a security program. Remember, we can set a goal of network survivability by requiring the network to transmit information even in the event of failures, attacks, or other mishaps. Network addressing and architecture can help meet these goals through policies that support diligent planning, paying close attention network addressing issues, and network expansion.

Network Planning

The level of network planning depends on the size of the organization. An organization with a small number of nodes can work around a network tied together using simple network technologies. They rely on the trust relationships based on physical contact. However, even small organizations might see benefit in using network architecture to provide access control.

Another way to think about this is to call it "traffic control." Network planners can help to limit access to secret or critical data by isolating the support systems and networks from general network traffic. There are many technologies to do this, including restricted gateways, firewalls, and air gaps. However, regardless of the technology used, policies can be written to ensure that network planning includes consideration for using architecture as a tool for information security.

For example, architecture can be used in a small company with fewer than 50 users with a very small Human Resource and Accounting Department. These systems contain sensitive information that, at least for human resource data, must be protected by law. Originally, the administrators placed these systems on the network and relied on creating a sub-network using addresses and network masks. Traffic to and from these systems ran on the same network as other systems within the office. The company wants to maintain better control over the flow of information among these systems. It is decided to partition the administrative systems from the rest of the organization and use a gateway to manage traffic. Figure 5.1 shows the network and the changes proposed. To ensure that this is done, you can include a policy like the following:

> *Human resources, accounting, and other administrative support systems shall be physically partitioned from the general network in such a manner to control the flow of information to and from those systems.*

Note that the policy statement does not say how this partitioning should be done. This will allow for new technologies to be used or a novel approach to be considered without requiring a change in policy. What also is not addressed is how information will be controlled. In my past experiences, some have suggested to include a policy statement that would mandate some type of filtering or routing requirements. I would rather leave that as an implementation detail because they can be changed with technology more easily than it would be to update the policy.

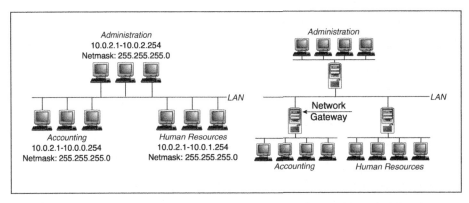

Figure 5.1 A network using subnets that are reconfigured to partition administrative systems. Note that the reconfigured network does not require specific addresses.

Network Addressing

There are no magic formulas to using network addressing for information security. There is certain protection that hiding or masking network addresses can give you. One of the key pieces of information someone can use to determine a weakness in a network is accessing to the list of valid addresses. With the valid addresses, someone can more easily pinpoint which systems might be active and narrow the attack. There are two ways to mitigate this problem: through domain name service configuration and network address translation.

Domain Name Service Configuration

The domain name service (DNS) is used to translate system names to numeric addresses. It also can be used to reverse-translate numeric addresses to system names. After someone knows names or addresses, DNS can be used to translate them to something meaningful. Although many people might think of this as a benign form of attack, one can gain a great deal of information from the names. For instance, it is common practice to name systems something meaningful. This is why many web servers have the name *www*. However, if I have the addresses for your organization's network and any address mapping points to systems named *hr* or *acct*, I can start looking at penetrating those systems looking for information. It also can permit attackers to determine your network architecture. Allowing this information to be seen by external users could provide information about the structure of your organization, regardless of its size and scope.

When I worked with a company of fewer than 100 users who maintained an open environment, they discovered that a system named *central* was penetrated several times by Internet users. This system was their "central server" and contained a lot of information about the company. Even after the system was partitioned from the network and router and rules were written to only allow internal users to access its resources, the attempts to attack this system continued. After working with the company to rename and change the addresses for many servers, we created a 2-DNS system.

The main reason we created this 2-DNS system was to provide name translation services for internal users with meaningful names, and the other was to provide standard DNS translations with "sanitized" names for the Internet. In this dual DNS approach, the internal name server would be inaccessible from the Internet and installed with system names that would be meaningful for the organization's users. The organization's systems would be configured to use that name server for address translation. The second would be installed so that it was accessible from the Internet and provided a different set of names for the public. Figure 5.2 shows how this would look.

Some smaller organizations outsource their Internet connectivity and do not have easy access to their DNS entries. This is not a problem as long as an administrator can request that changes be made. In any case, it could be advantageous to create a policy that would create a public façade that does not provide any more information than necessary. This could make your policy read

Network name services shall be configured to provide Internet users with generic names to accessible internal systems while serving meaningful names to internal, organizational users.

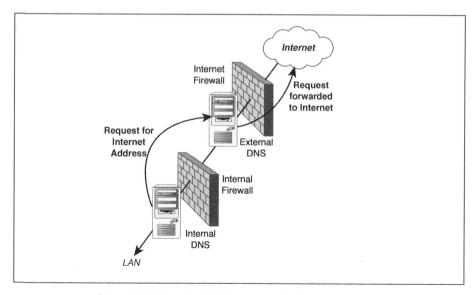

Figure 5.2 Using dual DNS systems to hide internal names.

There are many issues that an organization must consider before undergoing such a change. Some of these include how the internal DNS will translate Internet-based addresses for internal users, naming conventions, and accessibility to each DNS system. There are others. You should consider the ramifications of such a policy on the implementation. Just because I dedicated several paragraphs to this topic, I am not endorsing this as the best path for your organization—make sure it makes sense in your environment.

Network Address Translation

Another way to hide the configuration of the internal network is by using one address for internal systems but translate them when accessing the Internet or other external networks. The mechanism to do this is called Network Address Translation (NAT). The basic function of NAT is to use one addressing mechanism within the organization's network that would be translated to another address before being sent to the Internet.

Why Network Address Translation

When Internet usage exploded in the early 1990s, it was recognized that the growth would cause the number of available addresses to run out more quickly than expected. In an attempt to slow the growth, the Internet Engineering Task Force (IETF) published RFC 1631, *The IP Network Address Translator (NAT)*. This document explained how to create a network using the addresses set aside for nonregistered systems that could be translated into registered or "real" addresses routed over the Internet. Since the release of this RFC, security professionals have touted NAT's ability to hide network mapping and scalability without changing the organization's public face or the public's knowledge of the organization's supporting infrastructure.

One common use for NAT is to assign network addresses to the organization's systems that are not used on the Internet from a block set aside for private networks that will be translated to a legal address. These private network addresses are:

- *10.0.0.0–10.255.255.255.* A single Class A Address Block.
- *172.16.0.0–172.31.255.255.* 16 contiguous Class B Address Blocks.
- *192.168.0.0–192.168.255.255.* 255 contiguous Class C Address Blocks.

When using NAT, the user would access the Internet as normal, but the private network address would be translated by a system that maintains this connection but will translate the address before transmission (see Figure 5.3). NAT devices do not proxy sessions. However, it might be helpful to think of NAT as a proxy service.

NAT may not be the best solution for every organization. One problem is if your network grows, you may not have enough legal addresses to access the Internet. The use of NAT requires careful consideration by network managers. But if NAT will help your organization, the policy statement should be made as general as possible so as to give network architects and administrators the most flexibility. It could be something like the following:

> *The organization's internal network addresses shall remain private. When systems require access to other networks, the private address shall be translated to a legal, registered address prior to transmission.*

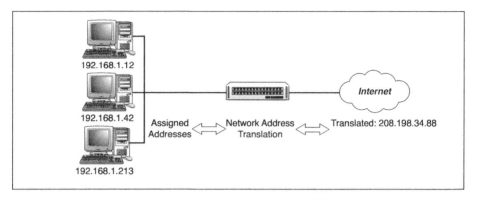

Figure 5.3 Address Translation using NAT.

Other Addressing Concerns

Some people are surprised by the number of considerations they need to take in something perceived as simple. But by having policies to address every important aspect of network addressing, you will spare administrators problems of managing different schemes. Policies in this area should consider how addresses are assigned. These considerations include the following:

1. Will the address be static and preloaded on the system or network device?

2. Will the address be static and loaded by an address resolution protocol, such as Dynamic Host Configuration Protocol (DHCP) or Bootstrap Protocol (BOOTP)?

3. Will the address be dynamically assigned when the system connects to the network?

There are advantages to all these schemes, but it is most common to use static or predefined addresses even if they are resolved using DHCP. By maintaining a map of network addresses, network monitors (both human and automated) can easily identify who is responsible for the network traffic. The policy to use this scheme could read

Network addresses shall be predefined for every system and network device and may be preloaded or resolved when logged in to the network.

The same consideration must be made for network addressing other than IP addresses. For example, IPX addresses in a Novell Netware environment or WINS resolution for a Microsoft network also have similar properties that would be covered by the same policy.

policies can be written in a way to include other address servers and controllers, such as the NAT device or DNS. This policy statement could read

Network address servers and those used to resolve addresses shall be protected in accordance with best practice appropriate for that device.

Policies for Expanding the Network

As technology becomes more flexible and pervasive, it is inevitable that the network will need to be expanded. When the network is expanded, it would be nice if there were procedures in place to make sure that not only the expansion goes in an orderly manner, but that an inventory of the network can be maintained. I spoke about this in Chapter 1, "What Information Security Policies Are," as something that could be done during a risk assessment. However, having this information available at other times can help maintain the network and provide a map for administrators to use to track network traffic.

Policies for expanding the network should be written as a general statement, such as:

Procedures shall be created describing any reconfiguration of the organization's network. These procedures shall include changes directly to all internal and external access points.

Although I would resist including specifics that would limit the procedures, I can see the merit in including a list of suggested procedures. If you decide that your policy should contain a list, consider the following:

- Adding or removing systems or other network components to an existing network
- Creating or removing a subnet
- Creating or removing an extranet connection
- Adding or removing an Internet connection
- Allowing and disconnecting a third-party access to the network

Network Access Control

Before talking about authenticating users to the network, policies on network access controls should be covered. Networks are no longer monolithic entities. In most cases, there will be one external access point—a connection to the Internet via an Internet Service Provider (ISP). Network access control policies will look at what protections should be installed at the entry points to the network.

Gateways

Gateways are the points where network traffic is transferred from the organization's network to another network. Policies covering access controls at these gateway points need to consider the nature of the network being bridged:

- *Dial-in and Dial-out access control policies.* Cover the requirements for authentication. It is difficult to hide a telephone access point to the network. Therefore, it is important to have controls defined. There are many policy considerations, such as creating out-bound–only modems for dial-out access. Your job is to write a policy statement that will call for sufficient controls:

    All telephone access to the network shall be centrally protected by strong authentication controls. Modems shall be configured for dial-in or dial-out access but not both. The Network Administrator shall provide procedures to grant access to modem services. Users shall not install modems at any other location on the network without appropriate review and authorization.

- *Other external connections.* Any access to the network from outside the organization. Policies can cover direct access from clients to setting up Virtual Private Networks (VPNs) and extensions to the organization's networks—known as extranets.

- *Internet connections.* Are different from others because people want open access to the Internet while allowing access to those the organization is providing its services. Policies for these connections are discussed in Chapter 6, "Internet Security Policies."

As with all policies, there will always be a request that violates access control policies. For whatever reason, you might anticipate potential exceptions by providing a mechanism for review. If your policies created an Information Security Management Committee (see Chapter 3, "Information Security Responsibilities"), you can require that they review exceptions:

    Any gateway proposed to be installed on the company's network that would violate policies or procedures established from these policies shall not be installed without prior approval of the Information Security Management Committee.

Virtual Private Networks and Extranets

The growth of networks have organizations looking for different options for connecting remote offices, clients, and making access easier to service customers or potential customers. This growth has spawned two types of external connections: Virtual Private Networks (VPNs) and extranets. VPNs are an inexpensive way to bridge two or more locations to the organization's network. Organizations create VPNs by connecting all locations to the Internet and installing devices that will usually do the encryption and decryption at both locations. To the users, a VPN can appear as if both locations exist on the same network.

Authorization of Services

Before continuing, it is important to remember that each of these gateways, or services, is an entry point to the organization's network. Any place where there is an entry point, there should be a consideration for some type of authorization for the data streams entering or leaving the network. One thing to consider is a requirement for authenticating those external connections to network services. This can be a problem for services that are always connected. For those services, there must be some considerations for how they can be authenticated to the network. In fact, transient connections, such as incoming modems, can have strong authentication requirements.

This section of your policy document is not to describe requirements for authentication; that is discussed in the next section, "Login Security." Here, you just establish the requirement for authentication. Policies regarding authentication standards will be discussed in the next section. However, to ensure that authentication is considered for these services, you can add the following to your policy statement for gateway connections:

Applications that require gateway services shall be authenticated to the network. If the service itself cannot be authenticated, services carried through the gateway shall be subject to authentication policies described in this document.

Login Security

All the precautions were placed on the network, the architecture supports the business plan and security policy, and the facilities are physically secure. Finally, here we are at the front gate. The *front gate* is where the user or the service identifies themselves and presents some type of credentials to request entry. The failure to have good login policies in place is like building the best nuclear submarine but using a screen door for a hatch.

Login Requirements and Procedures

The first thing that should be expected of any login sequence is to identify who is requesting access. Regardless of the protocols used, you need to know who is trying to access network services—or in some cases, who they want the network services to think they are.

So what are the user identification tokens that will be used for system and network login? In some high-security environments, such as the military, the user identifications are assigned based on a random sequence of characters. Other organizations prefer to use something that can uniquely identify the user without having to worry about how to create usernames.

If usernames can give away information about the organization, then random names can be good idea. However, by using random sequence of characters, you run the risk of having users write these names on not-so-well-hidden pieces of paper. If they are writing the names, they also could be writing passwords. This might beg itself to allow for usernames that can be easily remembered.

However your organization defines usernames, the policy should spell that out. For example, one company I was involved with used the employee number prefixed by a single letter to create usernames. Their policy could have read

> *User identification names shall consist of the 5-digit employee identification number assigned by the Human Resources Department and will be prefixed by a single letter.*

There are other policy issues that arise from usernames. Policies should cover the use of system names and the handling of default usernames. These issues arise from newly installed operating systems where the vendor includes a number of names for various services and convenience. Sometimes, leaving these usernames can cause security problems. Although most vendors have fixed this problem, having a policy will help make sure administrators address the issue before something happens. One example of a restrictive policy on system usernames:

> *System and default usernames loaded and required by the operating system shall be assigned a password different than what was loaded.*
>
> *Usernames required for services without login requirements shall be configured to not allow logins.*
>
> *Usernames for services not in use shall be deleted from the system.*

Guests and Other Users

It will become necessary to create usernames so that guests and other users, such as contractors and service personnel, can access the network. Even though they are performing a service to the organization, they are still outsiders. Policies for assigning usernames for these other users can include a mandate that the user read and abide by the organization's security policies as well as monitoring requirements assigned to the sponsor of these outsiders.

One common policy requirement is under what conditions guest usernames are assigned. One simple policy that has been common for the policies I have been involved with has been to allow an organization sponsor to request access to an administrator. The sponsor and administrator will together be responsible for review and compliance with the policy. This type of policy prevents a lengthy review process that would be required should the policy require a committee review, which is more beneficial when access is required quickly for service personnel.

So if you decide to use these suggestions, you can write a series of policy statements that say

> *Guests and other non-organizational users shall be given access to the network and its resources by an organizational sponsor and a designated Systems or Network Administrator. The administrator shall provide procedures for granting, revoking, and reviewing access to guests and other non-organizational users.*

> *The sponsor shall provide the user with access to the organization's security policies and procedures with the understanding that they are responsible for following them. The sponsor and administrator shall be responsible for monitoring the guest user.*

> *Guest usernames shall be assigned only for the duration that access is required. Usernames shall be revoked following the end of the access requirement.*

Login Banners

After usernames are given, policies might discuss the parameters and guidelines for login and authentication. First, in looking at the procedural guidelines, login banners are useful. *Login banners* are those tidbits of information that are displayed on the screen when the login prompt is presented. Banners can contain information about the system, including type of operating system or company information. Whatever information appears on the banner, someone looking to break into your system or network can use it as intelligence. Providing information on the type of operating environment can let the cracker know what vulnerabilities to explore. If the system or network is internal to the organization or this is not important to your organization, there is no need for a policy. Otherwise, a policy statement can read:

> *All login screens, displays, and other banners appearing during the login or authentication process shall not contain any information identifying anything about the operating environment.*

Banners Are Not Only for Logins

As you consider policies for login banners, it is important to remember that the banners appear in other areas. One important banner can be the line that greets you when sending mail via Simple Mail Transfer Protocol (SMTP). Most programs answering SMTP requests output a banner identifying the system and even the version of the software that is being used. A hacker can use that information to determine how to "test" your configuration for vulnerabilities. Although it might be a source of pride that you have a certain program working (especially to those who have configured *sendmail*), you might want to hide this from the general public.

One thing the banner can include is a statement saying who can use the system. These are simple nondisclosure statements outlining who is allowed to use the system. They can range from full-screen statements to a simple, single line that could read

> *Usage of this system constitutes agreement with the company's policies and procedures.*

In one of the rare steps across the boundary from policy to implementation, it is not unreasonable to specify the statement in the policy document. In fact, considering the review that the policy should undergo, including by legal counsel, it might be the proper place. So if you update the previous policy statement to mandate the usage of the nondisclosure, you can add a statement to the policy that says

> *Banners displayed during the login and authentication process shall include the following statement: "Usage of this system constitutes agreement with the company's security policies and procedures."*

Nondisclosure Agreement in Banners

The use of nondisclosure banners is not a requirement, although many organizations use them to inform potential users that the system is restricted for use and that their actions can be monitored and recorded. However, a few courts in the United States have made rulings that say that because the login screen did not have such a statement, intruders were not intruding—but invited in. These rulings were based on trespassing laws used in the physical world. Although there are new laws that provide better tools for prosecutors to use in these cases, the fact that there are precedents that say otherwise and judges who are not cyber-savvy should be cause for concern. Ask a lawyer if these banner statements are required in your jurisdiction before problems occur.

Login Controls

Login controls are those that assist the authentication process. These cover procedure requirements for positive authentication (biometrics, PKI, Kerberos, and so on) as well as consideration for multiple or simultaneous sessions. Policies for positive authentication should not specify a protocol or type of service, just that it be required. Keeping the policy nonspecific allows the implementers and administrator to use the best service for the organization. A simple policy statement could read

> *Login services shall provide for positive authentication that will ensure that a legitimate user is allowed access to the system or network environment.*

For some organizations, simultaneous or multiple sessions are not problems. In a typical workstation server environment, the networked system can initiate multiple sessions as required by the operating software. However, those using mainframe or other timesharing/single server environments might want to restrict the number of sessions a user can initiate:

> *Users with access to the production environment shall not be allowed to initiate multiple sessions.*

Login Reporting

There are two types of reporting requirements I like to add to the policy documents. The first is to log every login attempt in the system logs. Simple logging can be used to monitor activity by administrator inspection or an intrusion detection tool. They also can be used to trace activity of the system and to develop patterns of use. These patterns can be used by more sophisticated tools to watch for vulnerabilities.

The other policy requirement is to provide the user a notice of when they last logged in and from where. Although many users likely ignore this information, there is a chance that an unusual access attempt could be noticed. One administrator I worked with was helping a user who was having problems with her workstation. When he logged the user in, the "last login" message said that she was logged in at 4:00 a.m. on Sunday. This was seen as strange because she had been out of town on a ski trip. The administrator was able to take the information and determine that someone had broken into the network. Although having this was not part of that organization's policy, it was later added when it was discovered how extensive the breach was.

Setting Session Restrictions

Once the user is logged in, you might want to require a number of restrictions on the user's management of his or her session. If the user is working with sensitive information, you might want to have a policy in place that requires him to lock out access to other users or to log off the network altogether. Those accessing sensitive data should understand the ramifications of leaving their workstations unattended while still logged in or viewing documents. Their training should enforce the policy for keeping the session secured under every circumstance.

Other good tools for session restriction are restricting login times (for instance, during business hours) or mandating automatic logoff occur after an idle period or a particular time of day. Policies for limiting the amount of time a workstation or login session can be idle are very common. In many cases, they are combined with other session restrictions to create a solid policy statement:

> *Users shall log off and secure workstations when not in use. Administrators shall create procedures to ensure that unused workstations are secured by logoff or other means when they remain idle for a period of time determined reasonable by a review of the procedures.*

User Access Administration

Along with creating usernames, procedures need to be in place that guide in the over-all management of usernames. Administration of usernames consists of the procedures that guide the management of creation and revocation of those names. Other adminis-trative tasks include

- Handling of dormant usernames
- Procedures when employees are separated or terminated
- Removal or protecting "default" usernames
- Allowing or denying anonymous username (such as for anonymous ftp)
- Requiring the partition of user by group or function

Although these should not be defined within the policy, it can include a list like this to suggest that some or all of these be minimal requirements for administrative proce-dures. Regardless of how you write the policy, you should remember to word it so that you do not limit administrative procedures to your suggestions.

Working with Special Privileges

Some of the most difficult groups of policies are those that describe exceptions rather than the rules. Special privileges are exceptions to policy that require special handling and procedures to make sure that other policy and security procedures are not violated. Policies that work with special privileges have to be well crafted to not only allow the support for special privileges, but to outline how procedures should be created and administered. When you write your policies, you need to consider how special privi-leges will be supported. Please be careful as to how you write these policies. Even though I offer a sample statement, you should consider your organization's require-ments and tailor the statement to fit your needs:

> *Procedures for special privileges shall be written to ensure that they can be adminis-tered properly within the organization's technical environment. These procedures shall define how access requirements will be administered, managed, and reviewed.*

Passwords

After usernames, passwords become the front-line defense against intruders. You can be as careful about assigning and maintaining usernames, but one weak password can allow anyone to open the door to the network. Password policies fall into two cate-gories: what constitutes a valid password and the storage of those passwords.

Policies Defining Valid Passwords

Good policies for passwords specify that the passwords are difficult to guess. Although the concept of difficult to guess seems abstract, the generally accepted formula is that the password should be a mixture of letters, numbers, or special characters and not a word one would find in the dictionary. Another way to prevent guessable passwords is to maintain "social engineering data" for each user. This would be used as part of a pattern matching function that would prevent users from using it in their passwords. This information could include the names of spouses, children, pets, birthplace, anniversary, birthday, and so on.

In some organizations, such as military environments, there might be a requirement to generate the password for the user. Usually these passwords are created using a varying number of printable characters and given to the user. Unfortunately, these passwords are not as easily remembered. Users tend to write these passwords down, which can then be lost or stolen. If you have more control over the process, try to have a policy to allow the generator to make the passwords more readable to the users.

Another important property is how long a password is valid. If a password is valid indefinitely, a stolen one can be used forever. But if the password has an expiration date and it is compromised, there is a chance to stop problems at least when the password is changed. Although this sounds a little naive, it is similar to the concept of periodically changing locks to make sure that you know who has the keys.

When passwords are changed, should you allow them to be reused? One company I worked with maintained a database of the last 24 password changes to prevent me from reusing old passwords. Even though the policy was to prevent me from using the same password for two years, the assumption of this database was that I would only change my password once per month when it expired. However, because I used my account and password for testing, I was able to defeat the concept within three months. Whatever you use as a criterion, make sure that it remains consistent for all users.

Taking all this into consideration, a sample policy statement defining valid passwords can be as follows:

> *Each user account shall have its own password. A valid password shall consist of a combination of letters, numbers, or special characters; be comprised of at least eight characters; and remain valid for 90 days from when it was last changed. A password may not be reused for at least 24 months from its last use.*

Storage of Passwords

As a general rule, passwords should not be stored for everyone to read. Policies in this area would cover encrypting the passwords, using generated tokens, or even mechanisms to store the passwords of the systems or networks where they can be read using general access methods.

That was the formal definition. In most cases, you will not have control over the storage of passwords or how they are transmitted. Unless you are writing custom software, password storage is usually under the control of the operating system or software used. If this is the case, there might not be a reason to have a policy statement on storage. However, if you want to be complete, try the following:

> *Storage of passwords shall be consistent with the requirements of the system, network, or software in use. These requirements shall include not changing the required mechanisms to keep the passwords a secret.*

Special Passwords

During the late 1970s and 1980s, a very popular mini-computer was shipped to many customers with a username for the field service personnel set as FIELD and the password as SERVICE. This username was assigned permissions that allowed it to access the various diagnostic packages, many of which could do damage if abused. As I traveled between consulting assignments, I was amazed as to how many systems I could access with the default password. It is important that we reiterate the necessity of having a policy requiring administrators to change default passwords of predefined system users.

I was visiting with a friend at a large brokerage house one evening when his beepers and a few alarms started to ring. Within seconds, my friend and several armed security guards entered a room where someone was found slumped over a workstation. The unfortunate person had had a heart attack. To expedite his call for help, he logged in and entered a special password that told the network monitoring system that someone was being forced to enter a password.

Because the brokerage handles billions of dollars of securities daily, the policy of creating a *duress password* was created to prevent someone from breaking into the building and forcing a broker to log in to the system. If the duress password is entered, the brokerage's physical security services are activated. In this case, an officer was able to perform CPR until emergency medical services arrived.

Duress passwords are complicated because they have to give the appearance of allowing the user to log in while silently setting off alarms indicating where the problems are. To write a policy statement for this can be a simple statement saying that duress passwords are required or one that describes what duress passwords are to do without defining how they will do this job.

User Interface

Usually, user interfaces rely on the mechanisms of the underlying operating system or software. Unless there is some reason for changing the interface, policies can be written to require that they not be changed. However, systems that rely on enhanced interfaces, such as those for some network operating systems or public key infrastructure

(PKI) systems do replace or supplement the operating systems mechanisms with what is perceived as safer versions of the interface.

Depending on the environment, policies to govern the interface can say that the interface supplied by the vendor of the authentication service should not be changed. An alternative is to let whatever mechanism used for authentication adhere to other policy requirements.

An area where the policy can be effective is in defining the process of accepting passwords. To make sure that the process does not allow for the intercepting of passwords, the policy can limit the display of passwords, require a time limit to enter passwords, allow a finite number of failures, and require that the passwords not be transmitted in a readable form.

An interesting concept is what to display when a user enters a password. Some software prints an asterisk or some other character for each key pressed. However, if someone looks over the user's shoulder to try to see the password, the lurker might see the size of the password entered. By knowing the number of keys typed, there is a finite set of combinations that someone could try in attempting to determine the password. Let's look at it mathematically. If the password could be any printable character in the ASCII character set, there are 96 possibilities for each character position. If the password can be as short as six characters or as long as 10 characters, the number of possible character combinations are

$$96^6 + 96^7 + 96^8 + 96^9 + 96^{10}$$

This constitutes more than 6.7×10^{19} possibilities. Now, if I know that the user only entered seven characters, I now have much fewer combinations to try (7.5×10^{13}). However, if I saw the user press the "S" key as the first character, I have further reduced the number of possibilities to $2(7.8 \times 10^{11})$.

In many cases, you do not have control over what the software or operating system uses when passwords are entered. However, you can write a policy that requires the interface not to show the number of characters in the password.

Finally, the password interface should not transmit the passwords in readable form. One of the problems with the default authentication used on World Wide Web interfaces is that they transmit the password across the Internet in an easily decodable form. These passwords can be intercepted and used without anyone's knowledge. If it is possible, the policy should not allow for this type of password entry, especially for production systems. One method would be to require a one-way cryptographic hash. In this method, the hash function would turn the password into a fixed-length value based on the user's input. That fixed-length value would then be transmitted to the server where it would undergo another hash calculation, then would be compared to the information stored on the system. This way, only the hash is transmitted and stored on the server and not the password.

Using a one-way cryptographic hash is an implementation detail. You can put the other concepts together to have a policy statement read like the following:

> *Password interfaces shall allow users to enter their passwords without demonstrating any of the characteristics of their entry. Those passwords shall not be transmitted on the network in a readable form.*

Access Controls

Access controls are not necessarily authentication, but they do define who has access to the organization's resources. Access controls are provided different ways. The most common mechanisms are tied to those offered by the varying operating systems or software that supports the enterprise. This means that access control policies are tied to the technology used to support the business environment.

Access control policies should focus on where to use access controls instead of specifying to use them. You should look at the specifics so that a broad policy statement does not have to be applied to something that does not require control. For example, access control policies that restrict access to organizational intelligence that might be stored within a database should not be applied to documents that might be available through the Intranet.

So your first step in determining what access control policies are required is to understand where to use computer systems access controls or require username/password based access control. To do this, you go back to the inventory phase of your systems and note where these are used and how. From that information, you write the policies to correspond to those services.

One of the problems with this approach is that between writing the policy and the next review, there will be a new system or business requirement that requires its own access control policies. Rather than waiting for the next review, make each access control policy its own document and add one that says

> *Information owners wishing to install new systems or software in support of new or existing business requirements that require access control shall author a policy for that access control prior to installation. The policy shall be subject to the same review processes consistent with existing policies.*

After the new policy is reviewed, it is added to the other policy documents and becomes part of the overall security program.

Telecommuting and Remote Access

Every year the number of people telecommuting increases. Whether it is to support the single parent, the employee with disabilities, or as a perquisite, telecommuting requires clear strategies for making sure that the time used is for work and that the employee is as productive away from the office as he or she is in the office.

Another aspect of remote access policies is that used to give employees or customers access to the network from other locations. Usually these policies are for allowing dial-in access to the network. But new technologies might have you considering other access policies.

Employee Equipment Guidelines

Some organizations do not put restrictions on the type of equipment used in telecommuting or remote access. Those that do have equipment policies require employees to use equipment assigned by the organization. Otherwise, organizations do not create a policy in this area and let the Network Administrators define guidelines as part of procedures. Organizations that supply computers and equipment should have a policy that requires the systems to be used as-is and prohibits the user from altering the programs or configuration settings.

Remote Access Data Security Guidelines

One of the problems with allowing employees to work off-site is the security of computer property and data at the alternate work sites. Therefore, it is almost required that a policy be written mandating proper off-site security. This policy can require the same considerations as the user would provide on-site.

Some organizations might require auditing of off-site work locations. Although I have not seen this policy, I have heard that this can be required by the federal government of contractors to make sure national security requirements are maintained.

In addition to the security issues are the intellectual property rights of all work performed on behalf of the organization. To protect the organization's rights to those information assets, a policy adding the ownership of those properties to the intellectual property program might be a wise idea.

Employee Responsibilities

In a perfect world we can trust that all employees will do what is right and honorable with their work environment. Because we live in the real world, the one security issue we have to worry about is that the employee is actually working and maintains the company's policies and procedures while working off-site. One way to say this is to use a statement like the following:

> *The employee accessing the organization's network remotely shall abide by security policies and procedures to protect the organization's equipment, data, and network access as if they were working on premises.*

However, this might not be enough. Those working off-site also need to be concerned about remote monitoring procedures, software licensing, backups, and other procedures that the organization might use to maintain the organization's facilities. To strengthen this policy statement, the following can be added:

> *When working off-site, users shall use only properly licensed software, submit to pro-scribed backup procedures, and comply with all operating procedures.*

Telecommuting and Remote Access Facilities

Finally, the policies should explain how the organization wants to secure the facilities used by telecommuters that access the network. Typically, these are policies that govern the modems and the telephone lines that connect the modems to the world. However, with new technologies, the organization can consider allowing access using the Internet.

Dial-Up Security

From a policy point of view, modem management is similar to managing other network access points. Modems are entry points into the network; and whatever is decided on policy, the overall security program should remember that the incoming call is not necessarily a legitimate user dialing in.

The first consideration is the management of telephone numbers. Typically, most companies do not publish the numbers used by modems. However, I have seen it done by a company that wanted to make sure that customers are able to contact their representatives at any time. As a result, the phonebook was published with listings for "MODEM 1," "MODEM 2," and so on. Shortly after this was discovered, the company found an unusual call volume to those modem lines. Even though some might think that this is common sense, you should consider including a statement that reads

> *The telephone numbers used on incoming modem lines shall not be published in any directory that may be accessed by anyone other than those authorized for access.*

Another policy to help secure the modem pool would be to require a periodic change of telephone numbers. I have seen companies with strict access and security requirements change these access numbers following the turnover of several employees or the termination of projects. However, this type of policy has a big management impact. Not only are the numbers changed, but also those who need to know about the changes must be notified. Additionally, there should be concerns that the numbers are truly from a pool of known, inactive numbers. The logistics might be so complicated that this type of policy is not feasible in most environments.

In addition to typical access controls, you might want to consider extending the authentication system to require an additional step when connecting to the network via the modems. One example would be for modem users to use a one-time password or token mechanism. However, this is not the only way to make sure that the remote user has accessed the network legitimately. Before writing this policy, make sure you know what technologies are being used in your environment. This is usually obtained as part of the inventory process. Even if there are no extended authentication systems in place, the policy should reflect what is in place or should just describe a general extended access policy, leaving the details to the administrator:

> *Those accessing the network through dial-up modems shall be required to undergo an additional authentication step in order to be granted access.*

Tunneling Through the Internet

Although there have been many advances that have made accessing the network through the Internet safer, organizations might want to avoid using the Internet until the protocols and tools make it secure. But if it is part of your organization's business plan, you might want to write a policy that sets minimum requirements for securing the connection. One possible policy is to require that communications between the user and the network be encrypted. Another could require an authentication for Internet users similar to those used by dial-in users. Whatever the requirements, make sure the policy does not prevent administrators from changing the procedures when new technologies make tunneling through the Internet safer.

Summary

Network security is not necessarily securing the Internet but securing every network connection and interface. This includes establishing the relationship between the information and the requester. The basis of access control is authentication. Authentication is the front gate to any system or network where the information requestor is given permission to enter based on credentials. We try to mitigate problems by using network architecture as a security tool along with various methods of authentication.

1. Network addressing and architecture:

   - Policies that call for using network planning as a security tool will guide network architects to isolate systems with secret or critical data so that access can be better controlled.

   - Network addressing policies cover how much information on the configuration of the network is published outside of the organization. The DNS should be configured to hide names from the outside and Network Address Translation (NAT) for hiding addressing.

   - Policies should mandate procedures for expanding the network.

   - Issues such as static and dynamic addresses and other types of address resolvers also should be included in network addressing policies.

2. Network access control:

   - Gateways are defined as the location where the traffic to and from the organization's network is transferred to another network. Even though polices are supposed to be generic statements, you could be writing policies for Internet connections, dial-up/dial-in access, and other external connections.

   - Virtual Private Networks (VPNs) and extranets describe how the organization's network uses public network. These policies look to make sure that proper safeguards are taken.

   - Policies can be written to require that all gateway services are authenticated to the network or that services passing through those gateways are authenticated. Policies should give special considerations for services with no or weak authentication requirements.

3. Login security:

   - Usernames

     - Usernames identify who or what is accessing the system—or pretending to access the system. Usernames can be a source of information, so it might be wise to have usernames reflect the name of the user rather than the user's function. Policies should include what to do with system usernames preloaded with the operating system.

     - Guest and non-organizational usernames should be watched carefully. Policies for issuing them can include monitoring and expiration requirements.

     - Login banners might seem benign, but they can provide information about the operating environment that can then provide information to someone looking to break into your system and network. Policies can be written to limit the information provided as well as add a simple nondisclosure statement.

     - Policies should include considerations for multiple/simultaneous sessions and requirements for positive identification systems.

     - Logging of both successful and unsuccessful login attempts can be used by intrusion detection tools. Adding a notice of last login time and date so that the user can see it will create another level of potential reporting of security violations.

   - Policies that set session restrictions should include automatic logoff (time out, time of day, and so on), leaving sensitive information available without logging off, and mandating that those with access to sensitive information log off when workstations are unattended.

- User access administration policies could mandate a minimum level of requirements for handling the assignment and management of usernames. By making them minimum requirements, the policy guarantees that necessary items are covered by procedures but allows for administrators to expand on the list if necessary.
- Policies that support special privileges are finely crafted statements that mandate procedures to define access requirements and monitoring of the privileges.

4. Passwords:
   - Policies defining valid passwords look at the construction of the password and how long a password is valid. These policies also can prevent reuse of old passwords.
   - Password storage policy should state that passwords should be stored in such a way that they are not readable by the general user. Password storage is managed by the operating system; you can write a policy that would make certain that default security cannot weaken.
   - Special password policies should require changing or removing vendor defaults and should consider the use of duress passwords—when someone is forced to enter password, alarms are triggered to contact law enforcement.

5. The user interface for entering passwords should consider using the mechanisms supplied by the system or operating software. Policies can be written to cover what is displayed on the screen as well as protect the passwords as they are transmitted on the network.

6. Access control policies define systems or resources whose access must be controlled or restricted. Because these policies are diverse, it is suggested to create a policy document for each facility that requires a policy. To make sure that new systems have an appropriate access control policy, create one that requires information owners to have one in place before installing the new system.

7. Telecommuting and remote access govern how employees or other authorized personnel access the network remotely.
   - Some organizations optionally use policies to set guidelines for permissible equipment in this environment. Others supply computers and equipment to employees. These organizations can set policies that say the supplied equipment must be used as-is. The user cannot alter it.
   - Policies governing remote access data security should be written to require the remote user to provide proper security of computer property and data at alternate work sites. Additionally, these policies should establish that the organization owns all intellectual property used or created in a remote access environment.

- To create a sense of importance to remote access policies, one can be written to specifically say that the employee is responsible for maintaining a structured work environment and that he or she must abide by all remote system security procedures (software licenses, backups, and so on).

- Telecommuting and remote access facilities policies specify how the modems and the possible Internet tunnel are managed. These policies look at phone number management for telephone lines and extending authentication for either types of access.

6

Internet Security Policies

AS INTERNET TECHNOLOGIES HAVE MATURED, organizations have rushed to connect their systems and infrastructures to the Internet. You are probably reading this book because your organization has joined the online world and you have to worry about protecting yourself from outsiders. The problem is that many policy writers view the Internet security policy as the guidance to the overall protector of the organization's networks. If you have read the previous chapters, you know that I advocate several policies to cover all aspects of your information security program. The Internet policy is just one part of your efforts.

A common theme I hear when discussing Internet policies is that they are easy to write because everyone knows about the Internet. In many cases this is true. However, because technology changes so quickly and the tendency is strong for some organizations to want to try the next "gee-whiz" discovery, it can be difficult for some to write a policy that covers everything. Although it might be difficult to capture all aspects of Internet security, you can take a pragmatic approach to ensure everything is covered by your policy. Just like your overall security policy, Internet policies can be divided by technologies into logical groups. This chapter will divide the technologies into logical groups and explain how they influence policy development.

Understanding the Door to the Internet

A logical place to begin your policy is from the front door. Your entry or portal to the Internet can come from one of many technologies and require different hardware configurations. Once connected, this passageway will support many services that will allow the outside world to enter some or all of your organization's network as well as letting members of your organization access other networks. When I work with companies to create their Internet policies, I like to keep this part of the discussion to two very important issues:

- Policies governing how that doorway will be created
- Which services will be allowed to pass through that doorway

Architecture Issues

Policies that protect the doorway to the Internet can be as diverse as the technologies that can be used to connect the organizations to the Internet world. Regardless of the technologies used, the one constant is that the protocols used through this doorway do not provide any security. There are additional issues about tunneling protocols, but those will be addressed later in the "VPNs, Extranets, Internets, and Other Tunnels" section. Your goal in writing architectural policies is to ensure that security is a consideration while allowing the doorway to service Internet traffic without hindering access.

One of the problems you might encounter as you write your organization's Internet policy is that you will have to consider an existing architecture versus what might be "best practice." Although you might want to have the architecture restructured, it is highly probable that you will experience resistance in proposing these changes. Remember that policies and procedures are an evolutionary process and that you could accomplish your goals through incremental changes that can be proposed during future reviews.

Policies Managing Incoming Traffic

When talking about managing the traffic coming from the Internet, the first thing people think about is a firewall. A *firewall* is a device that helps manage the traffic by enforcing policy rules regarding what is allowed in and out of the network. Firewalls should not be the only consideration for managing network traffic. Placement of the firewall on the network and how the firewall does its work should be considered when writing policies in this area.

Although there are many ways to architect the connection to the Internet, I like to guide organizations to consider two types of architectures that try to keep Internet traffic from entering the organization's network. They are illustrated in Figures 6.1 and

6.2. These methods create a network segment that provides protection from the Internet and provides an additional line of defense before reaching the organization's network. This type of architecture creates what is called a *demilitarized zone* (DMZ) or secured local area network (LAN), which will provide this type of isolated network segment. Figure 6.1 shows a common architecture that will create a DMZ using two firewalls to isolate the network segment. In this architecture, the Internet firewall is used as a filter to restrict the traffic from the Internet, and the internal firewall provides extra protection to the organization's LAN.

Another way to isolate network traffic is to create a DMZ segment that routes the traffic servicing the Internet to a separate part of the network (see Figure 6.2). The advantage of this type of architecture is that it requires one firewall that will redirect traffic away from the organization's network. In either architecture, the purpose is to provide an area that services Internet requests—one that prevents unwanted traffic from entering the organization's internal network yet allows your users to access the Internet.

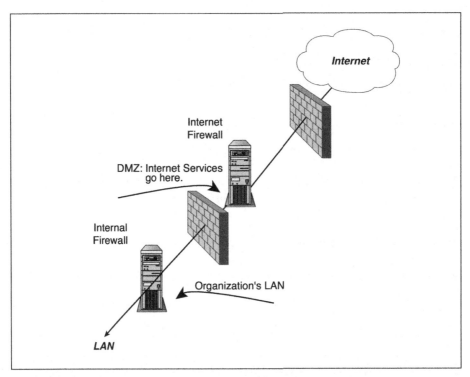

Figure 6.1 A network architecture creating a DMZ using two firewalls to isolate systems that service Internet users.

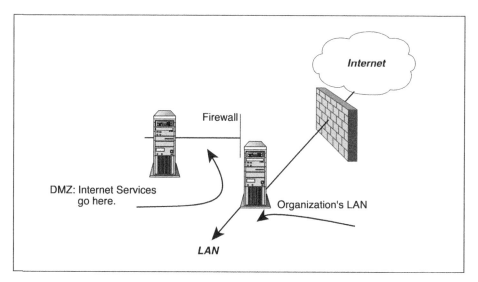

Figure 6.2 A network architecture creating a DMZ using one firewall to create an isolated network to service Internet users.

Architectural Options

The DMZ option assumes that an organization supports its own Internet service using some type of persistent connection. In reality, there might be different types of services that require different policy options. For example, if your organization uses a hosting service, then architectural policies might not be necessary. When you write policy statements for your organization's environment, make sure that they can be enforced—especially given that you might not be able to enforce the architecture provided by your Internet Service Provider (ISP).

Guarding the Gate

When thinking about Internet security, most people concentrate on the firewall. Firewalls, either as dedicated devices or packet-filtering routers, are usually the first line of defense in providing Internet security. They are placed at the various gateways into the network in an attempt to control network traffic. As was discussed in the previous section, firewalls can be used to create network segments that will support public access services while protecting the organization's nonpublic network from Internet users.

There is a tendency to create firewall policies based on how they work (see the sidebar, "Firewall Types"). For example, the organization that is using the capabilities of a router to filter Internet traffic has the tendency to have policies that require filtering firewalls. This might not be the best way to create policy because you will be restricting your organization to the workings of one piece of hardware. Rather, I tell organizations to resist the urge to create a policy based on the hardware and write one that will support the security program by the service (see the section, "Allowable Services," later in this chapter). By considering the service, it could give you a chance to redefine your overall security plan in a way that will not keep you attached to the old hardware.

Firewall Types

Typically, firewalls do their jobs by applying defined rules, otherwise known as the policy; by filtering traffic based on source or destination addresses or ports, inspecting the content of packets; or by acting as a proxy to better control some services. It is very common to use the filtering capabilities of the router connecting the organization to the Internet. Filtering firewalls are designed to open or restrict lanes of traffic to and from the network.

Proxy-based firewalls are systems that run programs designed to act for the user or the server when accessing network services. Proxy services are usually used when the firewall needs to look at the data being transmitted over the Internet to determine how to filter the traffic. Proxies also can be used to cache frequently retrieved data, and they can reduce the amount of traffic sent over your Internet connection.

Another common method is called *stateful packet inspection*. Stateful packet inspection is used as part of the packet-filtering mechanism except that the firewall checks the content of the packets for certain characteristics to prevent malformed packets from doing damage to your network.

Network Address Translation

Chapter 5, "Authentication and Network Security," discussed the use of Network Address Translation (NAT) as a security tool to hide the internal structure of the organization's network from outside users. If you decided that NAT should be part of your information security program, you might want to restate the policy within the Internet policies. This policy could read

> *The organization's internal network addresses shall remain private. When systems are required access to other networks, the private address shall be translated to a legal, registered address prior to transmission.*

Allowable Services

Better than writing policies specific to the hardware and types of firewalls, policies should be written to reflect the services that the firewalls are allowed to pass. By defining the services or even the anticipated traffic patterns, the policy does not tie your organization to a specific solution.

There are two ways to write policies defining available services. One is to write a policy saying that the services are to be defined as part of the administrative procedures for managing the firewalls. This type of policy has the advantage of allowing your organization to define the services that support the business process that can be reviewed by others within the organization. It also will allow your organization to add new services as necessary without going through the processes designed to add this service to the policy document. If this is the way you want your organization's policies to be, you can write a statement like the following:

> *Services supported by the Internet gateway shall be defined by a committee responsible for verifying the necessity of allowing the service through the gateway and appropriate business requirements.*

Another way to determine which services to allow through the gateway is to define them in the policy document. A number of organizations like to have them defined within the policy so that they have a greater impact. As you write policies for specific services, you should consider defining the services by protocol and whether the policy is for inbound usage (such as from the Internet) or outbound (from the organization to the Internet). Table 6.1 shows common services that can be considered for your policy.

Writing these types of policies means you have to understand the services and their impact before determining how to include them in the policy document. For example, there is a temptation to restrict access to User Datagram Protocol (UDP) services to the network. Many organizations do this because UDP is a connectionless protocol that is difficult to trace or even control. However, if the server that is providing domain name services is located behind a firewall, your policy must be adjusted to allow Internet users access to UDP port 53 to resolve the address of your organization's domain names. This type of policy can read

> *The Internet gateway shall prevent the passage of User Datagram Protocol (UDP) packets from the Internet into the organization's network EXCEPT for UDP packets attempting to query publicly accessible domain name services available on port 53.*

Table 6.1 **Services to Consider When Writing Policies**

Inbound Services	Outbound Services	ICMP Types
Domain Name Services (DNS)	Domain Name Services (DNS)	Echo
HTTP/HTTPS	HTTP/HTTPS	Time Exceeded In-transit
SMTP, POP, IMAP	SMTP	Host Unreachable
FTP	FTP, NTP	Need to Frag
LDAP	Telnet/SSH	
VPN and Terminal Services	NNTP	
	Streaming audio (Real Audio)	

Notice that this policy statement is for "inbound" services because it says "from the Internet into the organization's network." This does not restrict outbound services. Typically, organizations tend to ignore how their users access outbound services. However with this statement, responses from external UDP services will be blocked from reaching your organization's users. For some, this is not a problem; but if your organization is relying on services such as Network File System (NFS) or other network name services to collaborate with customers, your policies will have to be updated to support these services.

To some, allowing outbound UDP services seems harmless. In fact, if you search the Internet, you might find a program that can be used to proxy for UDP-based services. But the connectionless nature of UDP will still present a problem because you really do not have the integrity of a connection to protect the transmission. Many of these services have known vulnerabilities that can pose a threat to the integrity of network data.

Another problematic policy area is writing policies for the Internet Control Message Protocol (ICMP). ICMP is used to transmit error messages between network components. ICMP is transmitted on the IP layer and is used between network components. You can see the effects of ICMP when you use programs like *ping* and *traceroute* (or *tracert*). However, these error messages can be used to map networks, determine if systems are working and reachable by the network, and provide other intelligence to a potential attacker (see the sidebar, "ICMP Intrusions").

The problem with ICMP is that once you learn about it, there will be a tendency to write a policy to block ICMP at the firewall. If you do, you will lose the ability to receive `host unreachable` and `need to frag` ICMP messages. You need both to manage your organization's outbound traffic. Because these decisions are so difficult, I recommend to those I work with that it might be best to leave them out of the policy document. However, if you want to ensure that something is mentioned, you could include the following:

> *Procedures for ICMP services shall consider how ICMP services can be manipulated to create malicious traffic that could go unnoticed. These procedures shall consider ICMP service types that are necessary to manage traffic from the organization's network to the Internet.*

ICMP Intrusions

Understanding all of the problems that can occur with ICMP is beyond the scope of this book. One reference I like to use to show people the danger of ICMP is *Network Intrusion Detection: An Analyst's Handbook, Second Edition* by Stephen Northcutt and Judy Novak (New Riders Publishing, 2000, ISBN 0-7357-1008-2). It is also a great reference for understanding the technical aspects of intrusion detection.

Usenet News

I have avoided discussing specific policies for specific services. If they are not covered in other sections, I hesitate making them part of the policy document. I feel that including these details in the policy document will not allow those who want to maintain a compliant environment the ability to change something as quickly as requirements change. In most cases procedures can be updated in a few moments, whereas policy changes can take a while to write and review.

However, I feel that there could be an exception made for Usenet News. Started in 1979 by graduate students at the University of North Carolina and Duke University, Usenet has grown from the Internet's only mechanism for sharing information to what it is today. For some of us who have used Usenet from the beginning, the evolution is not something to be proud of. Although there are many productive newsgroups that provide good information, Usenet has become the catalyst for many of the problems we experience on the Internet.

Usenet is not the only service that fits into this category, but it is the most visible. Usenet's newsgroups require an organization to maintain many resources. Even if Usenet is maintained on its own server, the amount of disk space required to maintain a usable archive might be more than a small or medium-sized organization can handle. So when we analyze the information that is exchanged, many organizations find that much of the traffic does not support their business function.

After that description, most of the organizations I work with want policies that prevent users from accessing Usenet newsgroups. However, completely banning the use of Usenet can prevent your organization from accessing some very good resources. Your information security and system administration staff could benefit from having access to newsgroups where they can exchange information with colleagues as well as other valuable resources.

Striking a balance can be difficult. If you want to allow your users to have access to Usenet, you have to understand your options. Your organization can host its own service, access the servers at a service provider, or use an external service so that Usenet traffic will not affect the organization's network. In either case, the policy should reflect what is acceptable usage of Usenet newsgroups.

As an example, I will assume that your organization will allow limited access to Usenet news with no assumptions as to how you will provide access to newsgroups. The policy will allow for newsgroups that will provide some support to business functions and allow for the list to be amended at any time. You could write policy statements like the following:

> *The organization shall support limited access to Usenet newsgroups. This support shall be limited to a subset of newsgroups that can be used to support the business functions of the organization.*
>
> *A list of newsgroups that users may access shall be maintained by the administrators of the network. This list may be amended only by a written request. This request*

> *must include a reason consistent with the business requirements of the requestor. These requests shall be denied if it cannot be verified with valid business functions. A review committee shall provide periodic reviews of this list.*

Finally, if you allow access to Usenet News, you might want to provide training for your users. Just like email and other areas where users can include comments, they are a reflection on your organization. This book talks about user training in other policy areas. For now, you can include a generic statement like the following:

> *Users who access Usenet newsgroups shall first undergo training to describe the acceptable use of Usenet News prior to accessing newsgroups. This training shall include awareness for how the organization is represented by the user's participation in newsgroup discussions. Users also shall be instructed on the handing of the organization's proprietary information and intellectual property.*

Administrative Responsibilities

After you are done with the policies for connecting to the Internet, it is time to concentrate on specific areas that affect the usage of that connection. I like to start with the administrative policies. Besides being the simplest of the remaining policies, they are also the most forgotten because policy writers assume that they are covered in other areas. That could be true, but introducing them here will enhance their necessity.

Maintenance

The first responsibility to talk about is maintenance. Policies should require that administrators perform regular maintenance to maintain public data areas. As simple as it sounds, there have been organizations that have not specifically called for maintenance of web servers, ftp repositories, or other areas. Without making it a requirement, some have ignored public areas. In fact, a friend of mine went to work for a company with a small web server whose upload area became a home for hacker tools. The server was never checked and the web server was compromised to allow these files to be stored there.

These problems are not only the concern of organizations running their own servers. Organizations that outsource their Internet services should have policies that require these service contracts to include maintenance agreements or provisions that allow organization administrators to perform this type of maintenance. In either case, you can write a policy that mandates maintenance but not what maintenance will be performed. Those are procedures, not policies.

Outsourcing Agreements

Outsourcing agreements present an interesting problem because the organization might not have any control over the servers. It also becomes a problem for organizations that might support their own servers and outsource some of their services. You will still need procedures, but the policy should include a requirement that maintenance be included as part of the contract. One organization I wrote a policy for used a statement like the following:

> *Administrators shall be responsible for procedures that maintain the servers that provide information or services to the Internet user. Servers that are co-located or outsourced to other providers shall also be maintained by procedures agreed upon by their service contracts.*

Enforcement

Administrators also can be responsible for enforcement. Even for organizations that employ their own information security staff, administrators are the ones on the front lines. They know the systems, the networks, and they usually know the usage patterns and what to look for in the network. Even for smaller organizations where administrators do everything, they are the first line in enforcement. Although other polices should define their overall enforcement roles, I like to have a policy statement to reinforce the requirements. You can write a policy that says

> *Administrators shall enforce these policies in accordance with established procedures. Administration procedures shall include monitoring and preserving of information in a manner that will allow appropriate action to be taken. These procedures shall include, but not be limited to, preserving evidence for disciplinary actions for employees and legal action to be used for external violators.*

User Responsibilities

Policies covering user responsibilities should be used to allow the organization to define how they feel users should be using the connection to the Internet. Some of the organizations I have worked with have used this section to define the tone of their policies, especially considering these are the areas in which users are most interested.

Training

Users might think they do not need training to access the Internet, but the training I am referring to is not about access—it's about having them understand their responsibilities. Organizations must be careful about how the type of traffic they allow represents their organization. Perceptions are important, and that should be brought forth in your training program.

All organizations can have some form of training. The smallest organization can use a simple interview-style training program where someone talks directly to the user. I have seen organizations make the training part of their new employee programs, and others have rewritten their policies in an expanded form for users to read. How you provide training is a matter of implementation. First, you need a policy:

> *Users who access the Internet shall undergo a training program that will explain company policies and their responsibilities while representing the organization online. Users shall not use Internet resources unless they have completed the required training program.*

Understanding What Internet Usage Represents

When I help organizations write policies, I try to prevent them from including statements that should be part of the training program. One area I like to avoid is explaining what following the policies means to the organization. I am told that they want this included in the policies so that these philosophies are written in a document that is directly supported by upper management. I cannot argue with that logic.

After careful consideration, there are really two items that need to be in this section. First, the statement should explain that as the users access Internet resources, their affiliation with the organization follows them around. Whether it comes from the IP address or something written, their traffic, words, and actions reflect back on the organization.

The other consideration is what is being disclosed as the users access the Internet. In previous chapters, I discussed how the protocols could divulge information about the organization's network. All that work protecting the network could go by the wayside if users transmit information that gives that away. Additionally, users have to be careful about what information they disclose, not only regarding the organization but personal information, too.

These policy statements do not have to be elaborate, but they should be very clear in explaining how the organization wants to be represented. Here is one that I helped write for one organization:

> *Users shall be reminded that as they access Internet resources, they will be associated with the organization through the mechanisms of the TCP/IP protocols. Therefore, users shall access resources in accordance with their job description. Users may access sites for personal reasons, but this usage must be kept to a minimum. Of these sites, users shall not access sites that promote illegal, sexual, or other information that would be inconsistent with these and other organizational policies.*

> *When online, users shall be careful as to what they disclose to others. Users shall remember that email is not private information and anything they send may be read along the way. Further, users shall not transmit any information that may be damaging to the organization or themselves. Privileged information, as covered in other policies, shall not be transmitted without proper precautions. Users should exercise similar care when transmitting personal data.*

One thing you might notice is the statement of restrictions in the first paragraph. Even though restricting access to certain sites is covered later in this chapter, these statements serve as a reinforcement of what is expected from the user population. The rest are statements that support other policies.

Transmitting of Sensitive Information

In the last section the policy talked about not transmitting privileged information "without proper precautions." What defines proper precautions is how you construct this policy and your organization's needs. What your organization needs depends on several factors, including contractual requirements. For example, federal government contractors will have restrictions as to what they can transmit even within their LANs.

The other thing to worry about is the inadvertent disclosure of information. Users who surf the Net come upon sites that ask for online forms to be completed before receiving information. These forms can request small pieces of information; if many people visit that site, together it might provide someone with a lot of intelligence on your organization.

Idealistically, you want to write a policy that has the user request that a watchdog group within the organization fill out online forms or make online requests that fully control the message. But reality is different. I know that if I wanted to download a white paper from a company involved with information security, I would not want to submit a request to have it approved. For your policy, you have to write something that is possible to follow and rely on training and monitoring of the network to ensure that sensitive information is not divulged.

Some people see that there are two ways to mitigate this problem. The most popular way is to update the training programs to discuss these issues in detail. Another popular policy is to install content filters that watch everything that is transmitted to the Internet. There are technical problems with content filters that go beyond the scope of this book, but there are organizations that feel this is a necessary step. That considered, a policy can read

> Users shall not transmit any information that discloses the intellectual property of business intelligence of the organization. Users shall not purposely transmit documents or other data to customers or others outside of the organization without taking appropriate precautions. Appropriate precautions shall include, but not be limited to, encryption, transmission out-of-band, approval of the data owner.

Reliability of Information Downloaded

History tells us that the Department of Defense's purpose for funding the Arpanet research was to create a way for researchers to share information. From Arpanet's inception, its openness and data-sharing ability made it a popular medium among the technologists who used its services.

That really has not changed with the modern Internet. Various sites on the Internet store millions of gigabytes of software of varying degrees of usefulness for anyone to download. The problem is that there are sites that offer "less than safe" programs disguised as something useful. There are also some that are useful but contain bugs that can cause damage to the system and the network. Finally, there are sites that offer software designed to purposely do damage to a system or network.

With all this going on, there is a tendency to write a policy that will prohibit all downloaded software. However, if you do this, you also prevent users from downloading the latest web browser updates. Finding a way to prevent problems by creating a workable policy is a challenge. You might not want to be totally permissible, but you could say something that will prevent problems. One popular policy I have used reads

> *Users shall be allowed to download software from the Internet that will help them in their role within the organization. Users who download software shall do it on a system that is protected by anti-virus software and that software is up to date. Users shall not disable the anti-virus software while downloaded software is running on the user's system. If the installation of the software requires the disabling of the anti-virus software, the user shall perform a complete anti-virus scan of the system once the installation is completed.*

World Wide Web Policies

Here is one area where over familiarity seems to cause lapses in policy. Everyone knows about the web. Everyone uses the web and has an opinion on policies, but they are usually from a selfish point of view. The web can be a powerful tool, but it also can be a source for problems. My goal for web policies is to make the experience safe for an organization and not put a lot of unnecessary and unenforceable restrictions on users.

Web Access to Network and Infrastructure

Over the years, the moving target of information security is how the organization maintains its web servers and the systems that support web services. Every time new security measures are discovered, new vulnerabilities and hacks are discovered. Web sites are defaced, information is stolen, and the organization has to then deal with the potential of bad publicity over the incident.

Aside from defacements, there have been problems with stolen information like credit card data. This shows that there are weaknesses in maintaining these records or access to the infrastructure where these records are stored. If your site has been hacked, you know the problems.

There are as many ways to secure data and the organization's network infrastructure as there are web implementations. From a policy perspective, this makes it difficult to come up with a policy statement that will cover your systems. However, if you forget the specifics of the implementation, you might find something in common with all possible implementations that you could write as a policy.

For example, one way to protect data is to put the servers behind the internal firewall (refer to Figure 6.1) and define specific ways to facilitate communications between the systems. Although the details of this connection should be included in procedures, the policy can be written to guide the implementers in this area. This can be done with a statement that says

> *All systems hosting proprietary and customer data that support the web server shall not be installed on the same network segment as the web servers. These support servers shall be installed in such a way where only the web servers can gain access. The organization shall install proper controls to ensure that the support servers can only be accessed in a way consistent with the functions for which they are programmed.*

Another problem is the execution of programs, scripts, or other helpful procedures on the web server. Some organizations do not have problems allowing scripts that execute as part of the web server's common gateway interface (CGI) to run on the server. Others have expressed some trepidation with allowing anything other than the server serving pages to run on those systems. You have to be very careful when setting this policy because it will have a serious impact on the architecture of your organization's Internet service. Being too restrictive might not be possible for organizations that outsource these services.

> *Web servers shall only run verified and maintained programs and scripts that execute as part of the common gateway interface (CGI) with the web service. All other program execution shall be performed on other systems not associated with the web services where these scripts act as a proxy for that execution.*

Servlets, Applets, and Dynamic Content

The demands for web servers to provide more meaningful content keep rising as new technologies are created to help deliver that content. CGI was only the tip of the iceberg. Now with the invention of the Java programming language, small applications called *applets* started to help provide better access to content. But that was not enough. Technologies began to appear that allowed content to be dynamically generated based on the needs of the user. Small server-based applications, or *servlets*, and pages with embedded commands that are executed on the server began to appear.

Although these technologies have expanded the capabilities of web servers, they also have presented new security problems. First, these new technologies run on the same system as the web server. Bugs or other vulnerabilities can bring the server many different security problems. Second, none of these server-based programs have a single interface that can be secured through policies that restrict access to services.

Your organization should evaluate these options along with their potential problems and the policies being considered. You might decide that your organization's business model requires their use. If so, then you should ensure that policies are written so that implementers are required to verify that the safety of the service secures the interfaces to privileged data.

Security and Maintenance of CGI and Other Support Programs

We spoke about the strength that the web server has for delivering dynamic content through various interfaces. These interfaces are programmed using scripts, embedded commands, or programming languages that all have certain problems when trying to secure servers. The biggest danger is that these programs might have bugs, logic errors, or present other problems that are inherent with the language. Scripting languages present commands that are executed by external programs, which themselves might have bugs, security holes, or undocumented features that can cause a lapse in security.

In these times when development cycles are said to occur in "Internet time," there seems to be a lot of problems that crop up in user-maintained and vendor-supplied programs. Without delving into philosophies of software development, policies must consider the place for proper practices with the requirement to have software deployed "yesterday." They also should not intrude on software development policies.

When writing policies for these support programs, there are two areas I am concerned with:

- Reviewing all installed software for all potential problems
- The secure use of these features

Review of programs for bugs and security holes is usually an essential process of software development, but there has been a tendency to deploy software before it is properly tested. By creating a policy forcing a review, you hope that process owners will take a little extra time to ensure there are no problems from these programs. This policy can read

> *Support programs for web servers shall undergo a thorough review of all components. This review shall examine the operational characteristic of these programs for the unexpected results from flaws. Additionally, reviews also shall consider the ramifications to security of the system and network.*

Now you need to concern yourself with the features themselves. There are two aspects to worry about. First, if the feature is not being used, it should not be loaded or it should be configured so that the server does not use them. The other problem is that when those features are used, you have to worry about security problems found by security research groups, the vendors, and attackers. Sometimes, it seems that there are weekly warnings announcing security holes for their servers or content-generating programs.

Policies for these areas are difficult to maneuver. If your organization outsources its web servers, you might not be allowed to fix these potential problems. You might be able to create contractual agreements to coincide with your policy, but it does not get easier if your organization runs its own web servers. Your administrators cannot just install new patches or change configuration without making sure the updates will not cause the server or software to malfunction or worse, crash.

There are too many options to show just one policy statement for these problems. In the following, I extracted the essential theme from several policies to come up with one generic statement. I suggest your organization use the following example as a guide to constructing your policy, not as an example:

> *Web servers shall be installed with and configured to only provide the services neces-*
> *sary to support the operating environment. Administrators shall monitor appropriate*
> *security warning services for vulnerabilities reported on installed components.*
> *Administrators shall work with programmers and data owners to test and incorporate*
> *patches for installed components.*

Content Enhancers

Content enhancers are the scripting and programming languages that are called *run anywhere enhancers*. Scripts and applets are downloaded from the server to enhance the user's interaction with the content. The problem is that there has been security vulnerabilities found within the browsers that support these services. The problems have led to some organizations blocking their usage from Internet servers.

It is technically possible to prevent these content enhancing programs from entering the network. Unfortunately, your users might not be able to use the sites that rely on these enhancers. Although the technology is getting better and the number of security problems has diminished, your organization should consider the overall impact on security in allowing these enhancers into the network.

Filtering Applets

There has been an industry war between the use of Java and ActiveX applets in creating content. Java claims to be secure while ActiveX claims that it can create flexible dynamic content. Although both have serious security concerns, both give content providers greater flexibility in what they deliver to the user. Both technologies have been used for customer support, creating chat rooms, and enhancing e-commerce initiatives. This must be considered before deciding as to whether or not to filter applets.

Content Control

Previous chapters have covered data ownership. The concept was that one person or department would own the data for a particular business process. This creates a chain of custody for the data and sets responsibility for its safety and security. The web servers should be no different. Even if your organization contracts its web service, someone in the organization should be responsible for the content.

For every web service, there are even more ways to deal with content control. Thus it is difficult to write a policy that will adequately cover every possibility. The problem is that not only should the policy cover content ownership, but also how to change and manage the content.

Privacy Policy

The most controversial aspect of web servers is what the owners do with the information they get from their services. Privacy watchers are worried that we are giving away too much of our personal information in the quest for content and convenience. It seems that everyone worries about privacy and looks for web server owners to show good citizenship and disclose how they use the information they collect. This disclosure is a *Privacy Policy*.

Having a Privacy Policy is a little different from having a policy for disclosure. The Privacy Policy is a public statement that explains to users what personal information is being collected and what the organization is going to do with that data. Because of the volatile nature of the Privacy Policy, I never recommend that it become part of the information security policy documents. However, there should be a policy to create one that is available for anyone to read. The policy could read something like the following:

> *Web servers shall include a Privacy Policy that explains what information is being collected and what the organization will do with that data. The Privacy Policy shall be accessible by the public from links provided by the pages served.*

User Access to the Web

Rule number one of creating user access policies is that you cannot trust the user. There are no other rules. Organizations have learned the hard way that users will visit any site, download any program, access applets, and fill out any form they desire if there is not a policy in place setting and enforcing guidelines.

It is very common to see an organization with policies that include content filtering. Content filters usually prevent the user from visiting sites that the company could view as illegal or, in some sense, immoral. They also provide content caches at the Internet gateway to enable faster downloading of information. Other possible content filters can prevent the use of content-enhancing applets.

Regardless of your organization's direction, your policy should explicitly say how user traffic to the Internet will be managed. You need to spell it out for the users more for legal reasons than anything else. You must disclose that your organization is monitoring the traffic or could even audit what is being transmitted through the Internet interface. If you do not disclose this information and disciplinary action results from enforcement of the policies, your organization could be open to a lawsuit from the employee. Following is an example:

> *Users accessing the Internet shall not visit sites that violate the law or could be offensive to fellow users. The organization shall reserve the right to block access to any site it deems inappropriate and shall maintain logs of sites visited by all users that may be audited at any time. As part of the content-filtering process, the organization shall be allowed to provide caching services.*

When I helped an organization that provided outsourcing services write their policies, they were concerned that the policies would restrict their users from creating web pages. They saw this as an extension of their creative activities and did not want to stop the practice. I was suspicious of this practice. How were they sure that someone was not abusing the privilege?

Later that evening I started to probe their network from the outside. First, I used some standard tools to find all of the servers that supported web services. This probe found a number of servers on nonstandard ports. Using this information, I started to reverse lookup addresses to correlate names to those addresses. I found that one of those addresses had an alternate name registered with the InterNIC. Using the newly found name and a browser, I accessed the site. What I found surprised the people I was working for. The information was inappropriate for the organization's mission and could be considered quite embarrassing.

Because we were in the process of writing the policies, there was nothing in place to allow them to discipline this employee. They were able to take some action, but not to the extent they wanted. This led to a policy that read

> *Employees of the organization shall be allowed to create unofficial web sites on the organization's network. These web sites shall be accessible only from within the organization. Users wishing to allow their content to be accessible from the Internet shall permit their pages to be reviewed by a committee chaired by the Creative Director prior to making them accessible. The Creative Director shall use these policies as a guideline for the review process and shall have the responsibility for approving or denying public access to the pages.*

This policy was created for an organization with less than 75 total users whose web servers were co-located at a nearby service provider. Because they issued this policy, they had no further problems with user-generated content.

Application Responsibilities

For the most part, data and process owners are not as technology savvy as their programmers or administrators. Even those who started their professional lives as "techies" now find themselves at the mercy of the applications they deploy to be reliable and work within the organization's information security environment.

Internet policies for applications should be limited to securing data and file transfers as well as authentication of those transfers. Other aspects of application security should be left to other policy areas, such as the organization's Software Development Policy for in-house–created programs (see Chapter 11, "Software Development Policies"). By keeping it simple, you can keep the focus on the areas of concern.

Data and File Transfers

Nearly every protocol provides some way to transfer data between users with varying degrees of security. Although every protocol will just transfer data, some do not guarantee that the data will arrive at its destination. We take it for granted that data transmission is reliable. In reality, it is not. Instead, we rely on upper-level protocols, program interaction, and human intervention to ensure data and file transfers is completed.

Further complicating security issues, there is the potential that someone (human or program) can tap into the transmissions on the Internet and can read anything that is transmitted. Commonly called the *Man In The Middle Attack*, the organization's data can be read by anyone who has access to the Internet infrastructure during the file transfer.

After reading the last two paragraphs, you are probably wondering where the policy issues are. The issue is not to create a policy that mandates protections. The policy should suggest that data owners look into the roles applications play in file transfers and ensure that the security of the data is preserved. Simply, you can do this with a policy statement like the following:

> *Data and process owners shall evaluate all applications to ensure that file and data transfer security is maintained as appropriate for their business process. Security of transmitted data shall include, but not be limited to, ensuring that the data arrives at its prescribed destination and that the data cannot be read by anyone in transit to that destination.*

This policy statement is written to be as general as possible and only implies the use of encryption to secure the transmission. However, it is enough to make those responsible for the deployment of applications and the dissemination of the organization's data to consider the ramifications of their decisions.

Authentication of Internet Transactions

With the popularity of web technologies, we are faced with old problems in new forms. Services delivered over the web use a model that used to be called *block mode transfer*. More common with older mainframe systems, block mode transfer is the packaging of a block of data from a screen, transmitting it to the remote system, then receiving a block of data in return. However, in the web environment, the connection between the server and the client is terminated after the final data transfer.

Authentication is the identification of the user to the system, server, or software package to authorize use. Authentication comes in many forms, but the common means requires the user to enter a user identification and password. The block mode transmission nature of web services presents interesting problems in not only authenticating transaction, but also creating an environment where the user does not have to authenticate every time the server is contacted.

Policies for authentication should require data and process owners to ensure that you know who is accessing your data. Not only does this include Internet users, but partners that might have access via Virtual Private Networks. And the policies should consider every Internet-based transaction, including web transfers, database connections, and terminal services. One generic way of having the policy say this is

Data and process owners shall ensure that the identities of all users of proprietary data are verified to be valid users. Data and process owners shall create procedures to grant and revoke access to these services.

VPNs, Extranets, Intranets, and Other Tunnels

The growth of the Internet and Internet technologies have created new opportunities for extending the organization's network infrastructure to include remote offices, customers, and even allow employees to telecommute over public networks. We create these extensions by creating a tunnel between the LAN and the remote site.

In networking terms, a tunnel uses the Internet as part of a private secure network defined by a path traffic may travel. Usually, these tunnels are encrypted to prevent eavesdropping, but encryption is not a requirement. After all, Point-to-Point Protocol (PPP) is a tunneling protocol. However, as organizations look to expand their networks across many offices or provide access to customers, encryption is employed to create Virtual Private Networks (VPNs).

Not every organization will need tunneling. For those that do, a policy could be a very simple statement that defines the basics your organization wants to use. This policy could say

Data and process managers who employ tunneling shall ensure the transmission cannot be read by anyone but the remote system by employing encryption.

Modems and Other Backdoors

Another way organizations extend access to their networks is through modems. Some organizations maintain modem pools with special servers that secure and maintain connections with these external users. Others install modems on special servers that give access to a minimal set of users. Regardless of the method used, the common denominator is that the administrators manage modem access centrally.

Security professionals see the central management of modems key to managing these transient access devices. This way, they can be monitored and controlled while continuing to offer the service. What they want to avoid are allowing modems to be installed elsewhere on the network. A modem installed on a user's system that is configured to answer the incoming call creates a potential access point for an attacker to break in to the network.

Users will often notice that they have the capability to install modems on their systems that run programs that then allow them to access their files remotely. These programs have well-known security problems that could allow anyone who connects to the modem to access the system and the network that system is connected to. Additionally, because these modems are not monitored, administrators could never stop an attacker before damage is done.

Other than denial of service attacks, the only problem that could keep administrators up at night are those that come with a modem being installed on the network that is improperly configured. If there were a requirement to allow users to connect to the network, administrators would prefer the policy allow them to control the access. They insist on policies that will prevent the installation of modems out of their control. In that case, a statement can include something that reads

> *Users shall not install modems on their systems or anywhere on the network without authorization.*

Notice that this statement allows for exceptions, but with authorization. For these policies, I do not define what constitutes "authorization." This is left up to the organization to follow its review procedures as guidance (see Chapter 3, "Information Security Responsibilities").

Not every organization needs to allow modem access to its network. Some may install a few modems and write a policy to ensure defined configuration and security standards are followed. Others support several modems that allow users to dial in, connect to a server, and authenticate directly to the network. Regardless of the organization's requirements, the policy should support the installation and the administrator's role in monitoring and maintaining the services.

If your organization uses a modem pool connected to a centrally managed server that provides strong authentication, your policy can read:

> *Dial-up services shall be installed and managed by the Network Administrators.*

> *Users wishing to access the network via the modem shall be required to authenticate to the network on connection. This authentication shall include a non-repudiation component.*

The statement does not mention the type of strong authentication used. By only specifying a "non-repudiation component," you are not tying the implementation to a single type of authentication. It assumes that some strong mechanism that ties the process to the user should be used. This can include everything from a PKI mechanism (see the next section) to token-based authentication. It is also flexible so that when biometrics becomes an affordable option, it can become the technology used without having to change the policy.

Employing PKI and Other Controls

You might have heard public key infrastructures (PKI) being called the next Holy Grail in identification and authentication of users. PKI leverages the technologies of *public key cryptography* (see the sidebar "What Is Public Key Cryptography?") to allow users to authenticate and exchange data in a secure manner. PKI uses digital certificates to verify the identity of users holding the certificate.

What Is Public Key Cryptography?

Cryptography is the science creating algorithms used to encrypt data for storage or transmission data. Encryption uses those algorithms to convert data into an unintelligible form. In basic terms, encryption uses a secret key, a private value, to perform a mathematical function on the data to make it unusable by the casual observer. Traditionally, the same key is required to encrypt and decrypt the data. This is called symmetric encryption.

Public key cryptography is similar except the mathematical functions can use two different but mathematically related keys. The functions generate two keys: One is kept private and one can be given out publicly. If someone wants to send you an encrypted file, he or she will encrypt it with your public key. Once encrypted, you can only use the private key to decrypt the message. This is called asymmetric encryption.

PKI leverages public key cryptography by using digital certificates that are created to include the private key that can only be verified with the public key.

Making network components PKI-aware is not easy. There are a number of commercial packages that can help, but none can make this a seamless process. Additionally, there are diverse standards for working with PKI.

Currently, the most common use of PKI components is through electronic commerce initiatives that are accessed through browsers. Because this is not considered a "real" PKI, I usually do not consider it for PKI-related policies.

Because the standards for PKI and the technologies are constantly changing, it is difficult to write one policy that will cover PKI. I suggest that if your organization does deploy a PKI that you write a separate PKI policy and procedures document. This will allow you to craft something that can be useful for your organization's security program.

If you would like to read more about PKI, check out *Understanding PKI* by Carlisle Adams and Steve Lloyd (Macmillan Technical Publishing, 1999, ISBN: 1-57870-166-X).

Electronic Commerce

Since the explosion of the Internet, the most common form of electronic commerce (e-commerce) is the buying and selling of goods over the Internet. However, have you thought about the policies and practices required in securing an e-commerce system? The problem many organizations have is that in their rush to stand up an e-commerce site, they did not seriously consider security as part of their strategy. This could put the policy and the process at odds with the e-commerce initiatives.

E-Commerce Prior to the Internet

Before the Internet, business had been looking for ways to automate the purchase of goods and services. In the past, services such as CompuServe offered ways for consumers to buy online while businesses created Electronic Data Interchange (EDI) for business-to-business transactions. Although these and other forms of e-commerce exist, we will concentrate on what is currently used on the Internet. They can be used as a guide to write policies for the other forms of e-commerce.

Evidence of problems has been well documented in the mainstream media. Stories of stolen credit cards, banks unknowingly transferring money to off-shore accounts, or even stealing goods and services are just some of the problems. Your organization might read these stories and wonder how they can mitigate these problems.

The last time I helped an organization write an e-commerce policy, we decided that a separate policy and procedures document was the best approach. They had the same problem many others do: They rushed their e-commerce initiatives and ignored significant security measures. In fact, while we were writing that policy, the e-commerce development team worked with the policy writes to develop a plan to update their services to be more secure and compliant to the policy.

Regardless of how you approach e-commerce policies, there are a few principles that should be considered. They are

- *Storage of Data.* This goes beyond where the credit card information is stored, but where the catalog, prices, and other important information is located. Can it be located behind a firewall? Can it be located on a secured system? Can it be accessed through secured (or encrypted) channels? These questions should be answered before writing the policy.

- *Identification and Authentication.* For every e-commerce application, there is a different method to identify the user and authorize his or her use to the application. Consider what best fits your organizational business model rather than best practice.

- *Securing Data Transmission.* Usually, the securing of the e-commerce transaction means installing a web site-capable or Secure Sockets Layer (SSL)-based communication. If this is your idea, will you use strong encryption or will you allow the site to connect to browsers that understand what has been classified as "export strength" encryption, which is not as strong? Is your organization going to purchase its own digital certificate? Will your organization allow users to connect to the site and use temporary certificates, which is good for general-purpose applications, or will it be required that a customer connect with his own certificate?

- *Processing of Order.* Where will the order processing logic be done? Will it be done on the web server? Behind the firewall? On a separate server? What about processing of credit card payments? Will they be performed through the Internet? Or will you be connecting through a VPN to the clearinghouse's server? The decisions made here will have an impact on the architecture of the e-commerce servers.

If your organization outsources its e-commerce initiative, you might not have as much control over the site as the previous list suggests. However, that does not mean you cannot work with your service provider to ensure your service is secured. Check your organization's agreement with the service provider. It might have a provision to allow you to audit its site to ensure the protection of the server used in your organization's name. You can use this to work with them on reaching your policy goals.

Summary

Internet security policies can be difficult to write because the technology changes so quickly. Rather than create one policy, the policy writer can approach Internet security policies by dividing the technologies into logical groups and developing policy statements for each area.

1. Understanding the door to the Internet:

    - Prior to writing Internet policies, it is necessary to understand a number of issues that will be affected by those policies. The first issue is to understand the basics of the architecture and how the firewall and network address translation can play a role.

    - The next step is to understand the services that can pass through this gateway. To understand what to consider, it might be helpful to classify services by protocol type and whether they are inbound or outbound services.

    - You should then understand the differences between application proxies, packet filtering, and stateful inspection at the firewall.

2. Administrative responsibilities:

    - Policies that cover administrative responsibilities should mandate that they provide a certain level of maintenance services and be part of the policy enforcement team.

3. User responsibilities:

    - Users might think they do not need training to access the Internet, but the policy should require training to explain their responsibilities outlined by the policy.

    - Policies that outline user responsibility should explain how the organization wishes to be represented as they visit various sites on the Internet.

    - Most organizations rely on sensitive or proprietary information. A policy should be in place to explain the handling of this information.

- As intoxicating as it is to download useful software, shareware can become a problem, especially if it turns out to cause security problems. These policies should either ban the downloading of shareware or explain how administrators should write procedures to handle this type of software.

4. World Wide Web policies:

- If your organization is hosting its own web service or outsourcing it where it has to access the organization's network infrastructure, policies should be in place to protect that interface.

- Security and maintenance policies of the support programs and scripts should address the review of these items for security and bugs. There also should be consideration for the maintenance and security of the vendor-supplied features being used to support web services.

- Some organizations like to have policies to control the content of the information on the web site. Otherwise, leave this up to the data and process owner to determine what is appropriate information.

- The most controversial aspect of web services is what the owners do with the information they collect. So that there are no problems, a policy should be in place to make it public the Privacy Policy that will be used on the web service.

- Never forget the user in creating web policies. The policy statement can contain a short acceptable usage statement that outlines the user's responsibility in using the Internet.

5. Application responsibilities:

- Application and process owners should take responsibility for the information being transferred and that it is reliable and is disseminated only to authorized users.

- Policies for developing applications can rely on software development policies or just mandate certain best practices.

- To access data, applications should be required to validate the identity of external parties on the Internet as well as extended user authentication for inbound Internet users. This should occur for all applications accessing organizational data.

6. VPNs, extranets, and other tunnels:

- Not every organization will need these technologies. For those that do, a policy could be a very simple statement that defines the basics your organization wants to use.

7. Modems and other backdoors:

- Another way organizations extend access to their networks is through modems. Other than denial-of-service attacks, the only problem that could keep administrators up at night are those that come with a modem being installed on the network that is improperly configured. Policies can be written to control where and how modems are installed.

- Those that do install modem access to the network should consider policies that allow administrators to maintain central monitoring and control of these modems.

- Because they can be accessed by anyone, it is a good idea to have a policy that mandates strong authentication to access the network.

8. Employing PKI and other controls:

- The most common use of PKI is through electronic commerce initiatives that are accessed through the web and browsers. Because this is not considered a "real" PKI, you might consider it as part of an electronic commerce policy.

- The standards for PKI and the technologies are constantly changing; it is difficult to write one policy that will cover PKI.

9. Electronic commerce:

- Electronic commerce policy should consider the overall environment that it should operate. The issues that the policy will probably cover are
  - Storage of data
  - Identification and authentication
  - Secure data transmission
  - Methods of processing orders

- Even if your organization outsources its electronic policy initiatives, the policies you write can be the basis of your organization's contract with the service provider.

7

Email Security Policies

WE ARE QUICK TO EMBRACE NEW TECHNOLOGIES when they improve the ability to communicate. The explosion of email is the most recent testament to that. But email is not the panacea everyone believes. Aside from its ability to improve communications, email can be used to transmit proprietary information, harass other users, engage in illegal activities, and be used as evidence against the company in legal actions.

Over the last few years, there have been quite a few lawsuits that relied on evidence gathered from email archives. Recently, in the antitrust trial *United States versus Microsoft*, the government's attorneys used archived email from Microsoft executives as evidence against Microsoft. This focused the attention on many organizations' policies regarding how email is used and treated once transmitted.

Email is the electronic equivalent of a postcard. Because of this, it requires special policy considerations. From archiving to content guidelines, organizations have much to consider when writing email policies.

Rules for Using Email

Email has been around since the birth of the Internet. Messages are sent in near real-time and are not that obtrusive. The recipient does not have to read the message immediately, so it is not as an intrusion like a telephone call. It also gives the writer a chance to word the message carefully.

But this time-honored transmission comes with some responsibilities, which should not be lost on policy writers. In fact, when creating email policy, I recommend that the general rules and guidelines that users need to abide by should appear first in the email policy document. One client decided that in order to grab the attention of the users, he would include a "Ten Commandments of Email." Using email policy statements such as this is a creative way of expressing policy that gets noticed. Although they are edited to protect my client's confidentiality, here are those commandments[1]:

1. *Thou shalt demonstrate the same respect thy gives to verbal communications.*

2. *Thou shalt check thy spelling, thy grammar, and read thine own message thrice before thou send it.*

3. *Thou shalt not forward any chain letter.*

4. *Thou shalt not transmit unsolicited mass email (spam) unto anyone.*

5. *Thou shalt not send messages that are hateful, harassing, or threatening unto fellow users.*

6. *Thou shalt not send any message that supports illegal or unethical activities.*

7. *Thou shalt remember thine email is the electronic equivalent of a post card and shalt not be used to transmit sensitive information.*

8. *Thou shalt not use thine email broadcasting facilities except for making appropriate announcements.*

9. *Thou shalt keep thy personal email use to a minimum.*

10. *Thou shalt keep thy policies and procedures sacred and help administrators protect them from abusers.*

Administration of Email

What your organization does with its handling of email is just as important as your users' usage of the system. The policies and procedures that are put into place can become subjects of lawsuits, grievances, or other procedures that could embarrass the organization or the users.

The ramifications that come from email, whether it is content or how it is handled, do not appear to be taken seriously. This is a real concern because of the high-profile cases and security problems with email. Email policies should promote appropriate due diligence for both the user and administrator.

As you might have noticed, this section assumes that your organization manages its own email services. If your organization outsources its email services, you can check the contract to ensure that the service provider can manage the service to comply with the policies. However, if your organization uses an online service provider, such as AOL, your policy will concentrate on usage and have little to say on administration.

---

1. These commandments are loosely based on "The Ten Commandments of E-mail Etiquette" attributed to Patricia McIntosh (`fyrewede@concentric.net`), which was sent to many mailing lists (date unknown).

Establish the Right to Monitor Email

The Internet's most ubiquitous application also can be its most dangerous. Email can be used to transmit sensitive data, harassment, and security problems. All these can be mitigated if your organization monitors email for traffic and content as well as archive messages so that problems can be investigated. If you are worried, you should consult an attorney to see what is legal in your area. Otherwise, the right to monitor is setting policies for the overall handling of the email, archiving user messages; and scanning can be the basis for these policies.

Handling of Email

A client was worried about its email policy following a lawsuit filed by a former employee. It was a small company, less than 70 users, and it was concerned about adding architecture information in its policy. After questioning this request, I was handed a copy of a deposition that was taken of its System Administrator. The plaintiff's attorney questioned how the system handled the routing of email and if that was part of the security policy.

I reviewed the deposition and other supporting documentation. I became concerned that even best-practice architectures could be used as evidence against an organization. The challenge I faced was to write a policy statement that would allow the organization to architect a system yet protect themselves from being prosecuted for those technical decisions. Following is what I came up with:

> *Network and Security Administrators shall architect the email system in a way that will allow the proper delivery of messages both within the organization and to the Internet. This system shall be allowed to use, but not be limited to use, proxy, forwarding, gateway, and manual services to operate this service.*

Although this is a very broad statement that could be used for any architectural policies, it satisfied the organization's attorneys.

Archiving Email

Do not take the storage and retention of archived email lightly, because if Microsoft had followed its policy, the messages that were used by the government would not have existed. This is not to say that I support using email for allegedly illegal activities; but if your organization is going to have a policy, it should be realistic and should be followed.

Archiving and retention policies have two components. The first is to say that email will be archived. The other is to define some parameters for the length of time that email could be archived. As with other policies, it might be best to defer the storage types and some of the retention lengths to the implementation documents. However, you should include some guidance in the policy document:

The organization shall retain and archive all email messages that pass through its servers. The archive shall be retained on an online storage medium. Administrators shall archive messages to an offline storage medium every six months and purge those messages from the online stores.

The organization shall retain that offline storage medium for at least two years but may retain it for longer periods at the discretion of management. The offline medium shall be erased or destroyed in a manner commensurate with its technology.

Some larger organizations, especially government contractors, could have problems with creating a single policy for archiving and retention. They might be contractually required to implement a policy that is different form the one you are writing. If this is the case, the organization can include the following in its policy statement:

The organization shall alter its policy to comply with contractual obligations on an as-needed basis and without policy review. These changes shall only affect those users who perform work for that contract, and the organization shall notify those users of the changes prior to their implementation.

Scanning Email

Over the last few years, email has been used to spread computer viruses around the Internet. To combat this problem, many administrators have installed virus-scanning capabilities to their networks. This can be good, but is there a policy to do this? In this litigious world, you would probably not be allowed to do anything with information gathered without a policy.

Content-scanning policies allow the organization to look at the content of the messages. For whatever reason, some organizations feel they need to monitor email content to prevent embarrassment or proprietary information from being disseminated. The problem is that content-scanning policies are just not nice. They read like the organization is looking over the shoulder of its users because they are not trusted. For some organizations that project a "family" atmosphere, I can see how the culture might frown upon this practice. For others, it could be a necessary evil.

The concept is to write a policy statement that will allow your organization to scan all email in a manner consistent with the organization's business goals. If your organization is scanning for viruses and other problems, the policy should say this. If your organization will be doing content scanning, then the policy should say it. Regardless of the policy, if your organization chooses to scan email, there should be something, such as a publicly accessible document, that explains what is being scanned.

For virus scanning, you can have a policy that reads

The organization shall scan every email message that passes through its server to check for computer viruses, worms, or other executable items that could pose a threat to the security of the network. Infected email shall not be delivered to the user.

Administrators shall have procedures in place for handling infected email messages.

When content scanning, one policy I helped write read

> *The organization shall be allowed to scan the content of every email message that passes through its servers based on a predetermined criterion. If the message does not pass the criteria, the message shall not be delivered to the user.*
>
> *Administrators shall have procedures in place for handling rejected messages.*
>
> *Management shall have procedures for enforcing these policies, including, but not limited to, disciplinary procedures for users or involving law enforcement for non-users.*

Finally, either section may add the following:

> *The organization shall make available the list of items being scanned at the server.*

Limiting the Size of Email

Email clients have made it easy for users to create fancy messages and transmit large amounts of data by attaching files stored on the system or the network. With each new file format, the amount of data filling network bandwidth increases. One well-known university estimated that over half of the email messages sent through its servers contained attachments of a newly popular audio file format.

The problem is not limited to universities. Some organizations are finding that users have been sending documents to colleagues via email rather than using network file servers as a single storage location. To manage resources used for email, some organizations have updated their policies to include a limit on the size of the file transmitted.

Email size restriction policies can be as simple as everyone being limited to a particular size message. However, there could be cases where exceptions need to be made. In one organization I worked for, a person acting as a librarian was required to send and receive large messages from customers. They wanted a policy that was more flexible than limiting everyone to one size. Their solution was to create a policy with a statement that said there could be an exception if reviewed by a manager. That policy read

> *Email messages sent to and from users shall not exceed 40 kilobytes in total size. Exceptions shall be made for users with requirements that cannot be meet within those limits. The user's manager shall review these exceptions individually.*

Use of Email for Confidential Communication

I cannot stress enough that email is the electronic equivalent of a postcard. Information that is transmitted over the Internet passes as readable bytes available to anyone who can read them. As the traffic passes from one network to another, the probability of your email message being read increases. Additionally, if your message ends up in the wrong mailbox, you can unintentionally reveal information that should not be released.

After the message leaves your system, you have no control over who can read the message or that it even reaches its proper destination. Because of this, some organizations create policies that do not allow confidential or proprietary information to be included in email. Others might have policies in place to allow users to send confidential information among themselves but not to users outside the organization.

Encrypting Email for Confidentiality

The third option is to have a policy that requires confidential and proprietary information to be encrypted before it is transmitted. By encrypting the message, it should be able to be read only by the intended recipient. However, the use and handling of encryption is not to be taken lightly. There are many issues, such as key management, key recovery, and export restrictions, that are beyond the scope of an email policy. Although encryption policies are discussed later (see Chapter 9, "Encryption"), you can include a provision in your email policy for its use. For example:

> *Proprietary information sent to users outside of the organization shall be encrypted prior to its transmission. The use of encryption shall be consistent with the organization's encryption policies.*

Digitally Signing Email

Another concern with email is that a message can be created to disguise the real sender. This is called "*spoofing*." Although it is used by those who send unsolicited bulk messages (spam), it also can be used as a tool in corporate espionage. In this scenario, messages sent to the organization's users look like they came from familiar sources in an attempt to convince them to return proprietary information.

Users can contact the suspected requester to verify that they sent the request. But the culture of email is so trusting that this is rarely done. The only way to ensure that the message is a valid request is if it was digitally signed. Digital signatures are part of an encryption system that uses the cryptographic algorithms to create a numeric value unique to your message. Like encryption, policies governing digital signatures are best left to the encryption policy statements (see Chapter 9). Again, you can include a provision in your policy such as

> *Any request for proprietary information shall be digitally signed and that signature verifiable.*

> *Users transmitting proprietary or sensitive information shall digitally sign the message to demonstrate validity and traceability to the recipient.*

> *The use of digital signature shall be performed in accordance with the organization's encryption policy.*

Summary

Email is the electronic equivalent of a postcard. Because of this, it requires special policy considerations. From archiving to content guidelines, organizations have a lot to consider when writing email policies.

1. Rules for using email:

   - Policies should be written to promote the responsible use of email that supports the organization's goals and business requirements.

   - Some of the items that should be included in the policy concern courtesy, content, general usage, and compliance with the policy.

2. Administration of email:

   - Policies describing the administration of email discuss the actions the organization will follow in the management of the email system.

   - Administrative policies should establish the right to scan messages passing through the email system. This scanning can be for viruses or content. Regardless of the scanning type, there should be a policy in place that says the organization is doing this.

   - Email policies might include mechanisms to limit the size of messages to prevent the overloading of servers and network bandwidth.

   - To mitigate other problems, the organization might want to include a policy that allows them to use proxies, gateways, and other means to aid in the transmission of messages. These policies should not imply that messages are being filtered or retained.

   - If email messages are archived, there should be a policy that outlines the basics for how this will work. This policy also should define retention periods and potential exceptions to the policy.

3. Use of email for confidential communication:

   - Policies for sending confidential communication include provision for encrypting the data before transmission and signing them with digital signatures.

   - Encryption policies are really not the scope of email policies. Thus the policy statements should refer the user to the organization's encryption policy for that information.

8

Viruses, Worms, and Trojan Horses

Hardly a week passes without hearing about a new virus, worm, or Trojan Horse that has infected networks of computers. These problems not only cost the company money in their aftermath, but there is a loss of productivity that can never be replaced. Although these problems primarily hit the operating system and software of one vendor, no operating system is safe. Remember, the first publicized worm was unleashed in 1988 and was designed to attack Digital VAX and Sun Systems based on a version of UNIX.

When writing policies, you first have to establish the need for protection. You might think that is not necessary, but it helps establish the requirement for these policies and strengthens their effectiveness. Then the policies should include how the organization will provide virus protection (centralized or localized) and rules for handling third-party software before discussing the users' role in these policies.

The Need for Protection

Some organizations feel that they have to worry about the legal implications of a piece of software scanning information on the users' system. Although you might believe that this should not be a worry, your organization might never know how policies can be misconstrued if there should be problems (see Chapter 11, "Acceptable Use Policies," for more on disclosure). This is not to say that you are going to have problems. But

Caveat to Traditional Virus Protection

The traditional approach to virus protection has been what to do with systems running various versions of Microsoft's Windows operating systems or other Microsoft applications. However, there are virus problems that can affect other systems regardless of the type of operating system. Viruses that appear in certain applications can infect every system it runs on. One example of this is Lotus Notes, which can spread viruses to UNIX servers running the Notes server as well as those running Windows NT. There are even proof-of-concept viruses for PalmOS-based devices.

If your organization relies on cross-platform applications, your policy should consider protecting all platforms and not just the Windows systems.

many corporate attorneys want a statement establishing the need for virus protection and the organization's right to mandate the use of anti-virus software.

One way to ensure that the disclosure responsibility is met is to ensure that the policy includes a statement that initiates the anti-virus program in a language that limits its scope to this program. Although there should be specifics based on the anti-virus program strategy (that is, centralized versus distributed programs), start with the establishment of the program. Following is an example of a passage suggested by an attorney:

> *The organization shall use all means by which to prevent the spread of computer viruses, worms, and Trojan Horses amongst its networked systems. These means shall be restricted to preventing the spread of these problems.*
>
> *Users shall participate in this program and not circumvent it in any way.*

On the Advice of Counsel...

An old joke says that if you put two attorneys in a room you get three opinions could not be truer when discussing the law and information security. Although I tend to allow attorneys to override certain technical decisions when writing information security policies, you should not be afraid to question their judgements on these topics.

One attorney told me that the biggest mistake attorneys make is on jurisdiction of the possible claim. For example, if the policy statement is going to read like a human resource concern, have them understand that any problems might have to be defended under employment law.

Some organizations prefer a policy statement that does not sound as if it came from a legal brief. Assuming that your organization will install anti-virus software on all systems, rather than using network filters, you might want to use a statement such as

> *All user systems shall have anti-virus protection software installed before connecting the systems to the network. Users shall participate in keeping this software updated and shall not disable its facilities. If the anti-virus software is disabled for any reason, such as the installation of new software, the user shall perform a full-system scan before using the system again.*

Establishing the Type of Virus Protection

There are over a dozen companies offering a variety of solutions to help keep viruses, worms, and Trojan Horses out of your organization's network. The solutions offered work either on the network stream, on each system, or a combination. There are others that will isolate attachments and mobile code segments onto a system where it will run the attachment to ensure it will not cause problems on the network.

Mobile Code

A new entry on management's Frequently Asked Questions list is "What is mobile code?" The concept of mobile code started when Sun released the Java language and operating environment. The concept is to write a single program that can run anywhere. By making the code mobile, as in downloadable from a network server such as a web server, a single program can be sent to any system anywhere.

Currently, the biggest use of mobile code on the Internet is to use this code to enhance the user's experience with his web site. But mobile code can be used to deliver all types of applications, including viruses and other problems.

The trick to writing virus protection policies is not to write a policy tying your organization to a particular anti-virus package because you might want to change it. Most organizations install a virus protection package on each individual system and force updates every time the user logs in to the network. Others use network facilities to scan traffic as it passes through certain checkpoints. Finally, there are systems that will scan email and test attachments on a controlled system.

Whatever the system in use, let the users know through the policy how viruses are to be handled. For example, if your organization uses the system that scans email attachments separately from the normal input streams, the policy must say this. You need to do this because if questioned while being sued, the disclosure of the organization scanning is necessary to prevent other accusations during those proceedings.

There are three types of policy statements that should establish the full virus prevention program. The first establishes the type of virus monitoring and testing that will be required. Then there should be a statement on system integrity checking, which will help the organization validate the effectiveness of the program. Finally, a policy on virus checking for distributed or removable media (for example, floppy disks, tape archives, and so on) should be considered.

Testing for Viruses

Consider that an organization decides to use a distributed approach to virus protection. (The size of the organization is irrelevant.) As part of its program, it purchased a popular anti-virus package that will be installed on every system. Administrators will install and configure the software that will include persistent scanning for viruses and updating of the virus signature databases weekly from the publicly accessible service offered by the vendor. The policy that could cover this can say

> *Anti-virus software shall be installed and configured on each of the organization's networked systems in such a way to provide constant scanning for viruses and periodic updates as defined by administrators.*

System Integrity Checking

System integrity checking can come in many forms. Most common anti-virus packages can keep an inventory of basic system files and scan those files for problems every time the system is booted. For other systems, there are tools that look at the overall configuration of the system and that also check the integrity of the files, file systems, and binaries in public areas. Having these kinds of checks performed regularly adds another preventative measure to your security program. If your organization does this, you can include a policy statement that reads

> *All systems connected to the organization's network shall undergo periodic integrity checking for virus infection of its operating system and support software. The period shall be not more than one month (30 days) between checks.*

Distributed and Removable Media

Another difficult policy area is the one that covers infrequently used storage devices or removable media. Both have a transient nature in that someone can pick up a disk, tape, or whatever media the data is stored on and carry it to another system. While this is a good idea, that user also could be carrying a virus from one system to another.

The difficulty with these policies is that different systems have different requirements for treating removable media. For example, a UNIX-based system will not have the same scanning requirements as a Windows-based system. However, you cannot assume that a CD written on a UNIX-based system, for example, will not infect a Windows system.

One way to meet this challenge might be to have a policy that requires the scanning of the media on the destination system. If you use this as a policy, you can use a policy statement that says

> *Users loading any data or programs from an external media source shall scan that media for viruses before loading.*

Rules for Handling Third-Party Software

An interesting side effect of the previous policy statement is that it implies that program installation disks also should be scanned. Although it is rare, there have been cases where vendors have not been careful and distributed their programs with a virus. When this was shown to some security administrators, most seemed to agree that scanning distribution disks is a good precaution.

Most vendors go out of their way to ensure that the media they distribute do not contain viruses. They want to avoid the embarrassment and liability when customers' systems are infected because of their software. Some even advertise their master copy was scanned with a particular virus scanning software before duplication.

Vendor software is not the only worry. Organizations can obtain data from many different sources that could contain viruses or other problems. Then there are the shareware and open-source programs people download regularly that may not come from reliable servers. Regardless of the source, your organization could have a policy that mandates certain precautions be used when loading data from a third party.

Because the loading of this data would be from external media, including the Internet, some say the last policy statement should cover the handling of third-party information. An alternative is to have a policy that mandates that third-party information be loaded on a controlled test system for evaluation before it is used. Organizations that use this type of policy can augment the loading of external data policy with

> *Third-party data and programs shall be loaded on a system that can be controlled and tested for viruses, bugs, or other malicious problems before loading on other systems on the organization's network.*

User Involvement with Viruses

Not only is being attacked by viruses embarrassing, but if someone in your organization were the perpetuator of the virus, that would be an even bigger embarrassment. Organizations do not want to be known as supporters of spreading viruses. A number of organizations have requested a very strong policy statement about being involved with viruses. Some have even requested that the statement include potential penalties for breaking this policy. The following is a strong statement I used for one organization:

> *Users shall not knowingly create, execute, forward, or introduce any computer code designed to self-replicate, damage, or otherwise impede the performance of any computer's memory, storage, operating system, or software. Users violating this policy may be disciplined or dismissed and will be reported to proper legal authorities.*

I have been told that the fallacy of this policy is that users are usually not "knowingly" involved with viruses. However, the attorneys I work with seem to think that this statement gives the organization sufficient latitude to discipline users who use the organization's systems and networks to spread viruses.

Summary

Viruses, worms, and Trojan Horses that infect networks of computers not only cost organizations money but also cost them the loss of productivity—which can never be replaced. Virus policies can establish the requirement for all users to protect the organization's valuable data through a little due diligence.

1. The need for protection:

   - In some jurisdictions, the policy might be required to have a statement establishing the requirement to have virus protection and that it is limited to those functions.

   - Another statement would include a message to the user that he or she should use the approved virus protection and that it should not be disabled.

2. Establishing the type of virus protection:

   - Virus protection policies should reflect the style of protection your organization is using—not necessarily the product.

   - The policy should communicate the type of scanning included with this program. This is to ensure full disclosure in case of legal actions.

   - To establish the virus protection program, there should be policy statements that cover

     - Approach to virus testing

     - System integrity checking

     - Checking distributed or offline media

3. Rules for handling third-party software:

   - Although rare, there have been cases where vendors have not been careful and distributed their programs with a virus. A policy can be written to mandate special handling of third-party software.

   - This policy can mandate that these programs be installed on a controlled system and certified before loading them on other systems.

4. User involvement with viruses:

   - The organization does not want its users to be involved with viruses. The embarrassment could damage the organization's mission. This policy should strongly state that the user must not be involved with viruses.

   - To make this policy stronger, some organizations add a statement on potential penalties that can include dismissal and cooperation with law enforcement.

9

Encryption

TRANSMISSIONS MADE OVER THE INTERNET SHOULD be considered the electronic equivalent of a postcard. Attackers have proven how easy it is to siphon this information and recreate user sessions that can be used to create profiles and to steal users' identities as well as other damaging information. The only way to prevent this type of eavesdropping is to use encryption.

Encryption has moved out of the arena of the military and espionage to become necessary technology for protecting the transmission of electronic assets. From Virtual Private Networks (VPNs) to privacy-enhanced email, encryption has entered the mainstream of technologies that affects everyone.

Encryption is a special technology that governments would prefer people not use. Because it can be difficult for them to eavesdrop on your transmissions, governments have placed encryption in the same category as armaments. This is justified by saying that it is necessary to control this technology for law enforcement and national security. These issues require unique policy considerations when you write your organization's information security policy.

Caveat Crypto

Because I write from my experiences, my view of encryption policies and laws are based on what I have seen in the United States. Even if you live in the United States, you should have questions addressed by an attorney skilled in this area. You also can contact the Bureau of Export Affairs in the Department of Commerce for more information. See Appendix B, "Resources," for more information.

Legal Issues

U.S. policies on the usage and export of encryption are controlled by the President (Title 22, Section 2778). Before the growth of electronic commerce, the International Traffic in Arms Regulations (ITAR) restricted both the strength of encryption that could be used in the United States and the export of encryption products. As the electronic commerce environment changed, there was pressure put on the administration to change its policies. Congress joined in the public discourse by introducing various bills to ease the regulations.

Starting in 1996, the Clinton administration started to ease these regulations. After moving enforcement of these policies to the Bureau of Export Affairs (BXA) of the Department of Commerce in December 1996, the initial benefit was that users could download web browsers with stronger encryption. For businesses, further regulation changes were necessary to make exportation of encryption easier, especially when large organizations were trying to create VPNs with overseas offices. Changes were also necessary to streamline the licensing and exemption processes.

Changing Administrations

As I write this book, we are in the first year of the George W. Bush administration. Thus far, President Bush has not made any policy statements that would change current encryption policies. However, that does not mean his administration will not address these issues. The situation has become even more problematic as a result of the terrorist attacks of September 11, 2001. Congress has begun to consider several bills that could alter public policies on encryption. Your organization should have someone monitor potential legislation public policy changes because they could have an effect on your information security policies.

Depending on your organization's requirements, you will have to know what you can use, export, or transfer. If your usage is domestic only, the United States allows any type of encryption without restriction (see the section, "Liability Concerns," later in this chapter). However, some countries have restrictions for the use of encryption within their borders. Before you can write your policies, you will have to learn about encryption laws of the countries where you plan to use them.

International Encryption Policies

International issues become more confusing when you have to understand the provisions of the Wassenaar Arrangement (WA) and how the various countries implement its provisions. The WA is an international, multilateral arrangement that outlines export controls for the type of armaments defined in ITAR. The WA was negotiated among

Figure 9.1 The founding members of the Wassenaar Arrangement.

33 founding members (see Figure 9.1 for a list of members) to outline the export controls, exchange of views and information, and technology transfers throughout the world. This agreement, approved in 1996 as a successor to the Coordinating Committee for Multilateral Export Controls (COCOM), is a policy guideline to signatory nations and not a treaty.

Although the WA is nonbinding, signatory nations have created regulations that follow most of its guidelines. This has not made exporting products into participating countries easier. On the contrary, because these guidelines are nonbinding, there have been controversies between countries with varying degrees of compliance. For example, Australia and Japan, known to have lax policies on various provisions within the WA, have come under pressure to update their regulations and enforcement procedures.

In the new electronic commerce economy, countries have demonstrated various degrees of enforcement on policies covered by the WA. The lure of new markets and increased tax revenues are the incentive to some countries to loosen their enforcement. Some countries have completely abandoned enforcement as a way to nurture an industry with such potential. However, these countries have been known to be pedantic in the enforcement of import restrictions. This dichotomy has upset the U.S. State Department, which has asked the Secretariat of the WA to mediate disputes.

The result of the actual compliance record of WA participants and the new BXA regulations has been a more open market for encryption products domestically. However, there continues to be some problems with countries that have not adopted the WA and obtained the licenses from the BXA for export.

Seven Exceptions to U.S. Encryption Policy

Regardless of how open the export standards become, U.S. policies will continue to prevent the export and use of encryption to the nations that the State Department lists as being enemies of the United States or those supporting terrorism. As of this writing, the nations on this list are Cuba, Iran, Iraq, Libya, North Korea, Syria, and Sudan.

Liability Concerns

To further confuse the issue, you might have to worry about the legal liability issues of using encryption, even if your use is domestic. The primary concern occurs when law enforcement obtains warrants to search your organization's systems or monitor encrypted network transmissions. In these cases, law enforcement will require the disclosure of the encryption algorithms and the keys so that they can conduct their business. Additionally, encrypted data is supposed to be safe from prying eyes, and the keys used are supposed to remain safe—including when being given to law enforcement.

Although not required by law, some organizations opt to participate in key recovery or key escrow programs in order to allow law enforcement to lawfully conduct investigations. Key recovery or escrow is a very controversial topic and beyond the scope of this book. However, if your work involves the federal government, you could be required to have key escrow policies and capabilities as part of your work program.

Managing Encryption

Even with the legal questions surrounding the use of encryption, it is a good tool to ensure the privacy of network communications. When developing your organization's policies, you should start with the management responsibilities of using encryption. For example, some organizations will require that management approve the use of encryption. Management, in turn, will be responsible for certifying its use only after verifying any legal issues. This policy can be stated as follows:

> *Management shall approve all use of encryption within the organization. Prior to approval, management shall verify that its use complies with all applicable laws and regulations.*

Compliance with laws and regulations can be limited to ensuring that the type of encryption and devices used all come from domestic vendors. However, if your organization is contracted to the federal government, compliance means that your decisions must meet published government standards.

Federal Encryption Standards

For nonmilitary and intelligence agencies, all technical standards for federal computing systems are specified in the Federal Information Processing Standards (FIPS) documents. The National Institute of Standards and Technology (NIST) maintains these documents and are the final authority when working with the federal government. Federal encryption standards are maintained as part of FIPS Publication 140-2, last updated June 2001 (as of this writing). Appendix B has more information about how to find FIPS Pub 140-2 and other FIPS documents.

In addition to management issues, policies can consider the physical management of hardware and software media used to support encryption. Just as physical security is important for the overall information security program, protecting the physical access to the hardware can be just as important. After all, if your organization is using a hardware encryption device, at some point the data either entering or exiting the device can be read by anyone. Some physical policies to consider include

- Requiring tamper-resistant hardware
- Physically locking the device that uses a real key
- Placing safeguards on the physical network, including physically protecting hardware devices and network connections to those devices
- Locking storage for software distribution media

If you have any questions, FIPS Pub 140-2 (refer to sidebar, "Federal Encryption Standards") also covers the physical security requirements of encryption devices. Though these are federal requirements, they are good provisions to consider for a nongovernment environment.

Handling Encryption and Encrypted Data

With all the consideration that has to be placed on using encryption, there is the tendency to try to write specific policies as to how to handle encrypted data. However, here is one area where you have to remember that the policies are supposed to be guidelines and that the specifics are to be left to the procedures.

Policies covering when to encrypt data are something that can be left to procedures. The purpose of policies in this area is to provide some guidance as to how to create those procedures. While considering this problem, one organization I worked with decided that data would be classified based on storage or transmission requirements. After a lengthy discussion, we decided that rather than inserting those classifications in the policy document, the policy would support the classification of data in such a way that if it did not work, it could be withdrawn. This statement read as follows:

> All data shall be classified based on usage. The criteria shall include considerations for the sensitivity of the data, where it is stored, and how the data is transmitted.

During these discussions, someone brought up encrypting sensitive archive data. I had learned that this organization was converting archived data from magnetic tapes to optical storage media. They began to wonder if it would be best to encrypt this data. As we discussed the concept, we realized that there would be a problem with key management and key recovery for each copy of the media. The complexity of the system became so great that they decided to strengthen the policies for storage of the backup media and include a policy statement that read

> Archive and backup data shall not be encrypted. Sensitive data shall be stored in a manner consistent with policy.

Finally, the discussion lead to what to do with the data after it is encrypted. After all, if the data is being encrypted, care must be taken to ensure that it cannot be read from the system. The organization began to worry about its old tapes and the online data as it was being encrypted. The discussions led to a policy that statement that said

All original data shall be deleted or its media destroyed after it is encrypted. Memory and storage used by encryption processes shall be thoroughly erased before being released.

This policy was simple yet explicit enough to allow those creating procedures to ensure that encrypted data was safe. When writing policies, try not to get too specific; if the procedures have to change, you might have to change the policies too.

Key Generation Considerations

One of the most important aspects of dealing with encryption is the *key*. In encryption, the key is the variable applied to the algorithm used to encrypt the data. The key is usually a secret value or has a secret component. It is important to ensure that the key remains a secret.

It can be difficult to write key generation policies without considering the encryption environment and the software used in generating the keys. Policies can specify certain rules that should be followed, leaving it up to the administrators to create the appropriate process. Rules that can be used include the following:

- The allowable format for generated keys: binary or plaintext.
- How the keys can be stored. This can include online storage, removable storage, and the storage of keys within devices.
- Specifying the allowable life of a key. For public key algorithms, the generated certificates can be created with an expiration date. Symmetrical keys might require administrators to work with users to regenerate keys when they are supposed to expire.
- Mandating that the key-generating algorithms and software not be made generally available.

Another consideration for key generation is the handling of key materials after the keys are generated. Policies calling for the destruction of key-generating materials can mean ensuring that memory used to generate keys does not leave any residual information that could be read by another program. Additionally, other tools, such as floppy disks that might be used to transfer keys from the computer that generated the keys, also must be considered in the policy. This policy statement can read as follows:

All materials used in generating encryption keys shall be destroyed following their use. All memory and storage devices shall be thoroughly erased or destroyed as appropriate.

Key Management

The issues of key management make managing encryption and creating policies difficult. Not only are the issues complicated, but they change depending on whether your organization is using hardware accelerators or software-only systems. There are also differences between symmetric and asymmetric encryption.

When there are questions as to how to work with technology, the answer is usually to use the standards. However, if your organization is using public key cryptography and trying to create a public key infrastructure (PKI), the standards are in flux, making it difficult to find answers. Vendors can provide guidance, but be careful as to not allow them to influence the policy in such a way that your organization is locked into their solution. For more information on PKI and its associated policies, see the section "Employing PKI and Other Controls" in Chapter 6, "Internet Security Policies."

From a policy perspective, there are three areas that should be covered in key management policies: disclosure of keys and key escrows, storage of keys, and transmission of keys. This is certainly not the definitive list, but these are the major issues that you can use as a start.

Disclosure of Keys

Regardless of the type of encryption used, keys will have to be disclosed at some point. If your organization is setting up a VPN, the network devices doing the encryption will have to trade keys when initialized or during required change periods. This will occur whether the organization is supporting the equipment or a service provider is supporting them.

Keys might have to be disclosed under court order. Law enforcement can obtain orders to monitor your organization's network transmissions. If they are encrypted, the court could order you to turn over the details of the algorithm used and the keys that encrypt the data. Although this could be disconcerting, there may be nothing you can do about it.

If your organization outsources services that use encryption, many providers manage the keys through key escrow systems. Providers will tell you that it makes key recovery easier. It also makes disclosure of the keys easier and anonymous to your organization. If there is a criminal investigation, whether against or involving your organization, law enforcement can present their warrant to the service provider, and your organization will not know about the surveillance. Although this statement sounds as if I am advocating hiding illegal activities, my concern is for the organization that is upholding the law having the ability to mitigate problems and even assist law enforcement with an investigation before being embarrassed.

Maintaining control of the keys is essential for maintaining the confidentiality of the data being encrypted. Although the policy seems very basic, specifying is necessary to ensure that that there is no confusion. Key management policy can read

Encryption keys shall be disclosed only when required for exchange or by law.

This policy statement does not address key escrow, management of keys through a third party, or disclosure of employees' keys when their association with the organization is terminated. These present real policy issues that cannot be addressed generically. When working with a service provider, your organization should receive a policy statement from the provider stating its disclosure policies.

Key Storage

Certain aspects of key storage cannot be controlled. Hardware encryption devices will have storage capabilities that are required for them to work properly. Software will have to have some online storage capabilities, including being within memory. The areas for policies of key storage are the backup and other storage of keys.

Key storage policies can cover how keys are stored, backed up, or stored for transmission. One area that always seems to be a concern is the storage of keys on the same device or media as the protected data. In one discussion, someone pointed out that storing the keys on the same disk as the protected data is logically equivalent to leaving one's house key under the doormat. This was an easy policy:

> *Keys shall not be stored on the same media as the protected data.*

As for other key storage policies, such as eradicating keys from media, most organizations have chosen to leave requirements unspecified and include them in their procedures.

Transmission of Keys

For any encryption algorithms to work, keys must be exchanged. Public key or asymmetric technologies have fewer concerns because the public key can be transmitted openly without worrying about compromise (see Chapter 6 for an explanation of public key cryptography). Public keys used as part of a PKI also can be exchanged through a certification authority that will not only store the key but also digitally sign it to certify validity.

Those using symmetric encryption must find alternate ways to transmit keys. When initializing links that rely on symmetric encryption to protect transmission, they must find an out-of-band method for transmitting the key to the remote location. When I say "out-of-band," I mean some method for transmitting the key that does not follow the same transmission path as the data. For example, using offline methods, like a courier carrying a floppy disk or tape, is considered an out-of-band transmission mechanism. Some organizations have procedures in place to initialize the encryption (or VPN) device before shipping it to the remote location. After it's initialized, the old key can be used to transmit the new key. However, if the old key was compromised, it would be pointless to electronically transmit the new key this way.

If your organization outsources its VPN services, the service provider will perform these management issues. However, your organization can question the provider as to how it will manage and transmit these keys among the various network connections.

Although these issues might never become policy, you can have a policy to review this information with the service provider.

For those who manage the transmission of their own keys, many express concern over transmitting them using the same methods as ordinary data travels. One organization that established a PKI arranged with the certification authority to manage their keys via a modem on a system largely isolated from the rest of the organization's network. The organization based this on a simple policy that mandated this out-of-band transmission that read

> *All management of public key/asymmetric encryption keys shall not be transmitted using the same network that will carry encrypted data. All symmetric encryption keys shall be physically exchanged and not transmitted across any network.*

Notice that the policy specifies no transmission of symmetric keys. This organization believed that if the old keys were compromised, then transmitting new keys using the old keys to encrypt them would be pointless.

Summary

The nature of transmitting data over the Internet makes it easy for a determined attacker to read your data. The only way to prevent this type of eavesdropping is to use encryption. Encryption is a special technology that governments would prefer people not use because it can be difficult for them to eavesdrop on your transmissions. These issues require unique policy considerations to write information security policies.

1. Legal issues:

   - The United States and other governments classify encryption technologies as armaments. Thus governments have laws in place to restrict both the strength of encryption that could be used and the export of encryption products.

   - In 1998, the Clinton administration started to ease encryption-related regulations. Enforcement of these policies was moved to the Bureau of Export Affairs (BXA). The new policy changed public standards on encryption strength and streamlined the licensing and exemption processes.

   - International laws are based on the provisions of the Wassenaar Arrangement, an international, multilateral arrangement that outlines export controls for the type of armaments, including encryption. Although the Wassenaar Arrangement is nonbinding, signatory nations have created regulations that follow most of its guidelines.

   - Although encrypted data is supposed to be private, law enforcement officials can obtain warrants to search your organization's systems or monitor encrypted network transmissions. If you participate in a key escrow program, keys can be recovered without your organization's permission.

2. Managing encryption:

   - Some organizations require that management approve the use of encryption. Management, in turn, will be responsible for certifying its use only after verifying any legal issues.

   - If your organization is contracting to the federal government, managing compliance means that your decisions must meet published government standards.

   - Policies can consider the physical management of hardware and software media used to support encryption. Some physical policies to consider include policies requiring tamper-resistant hardware, physical locking capabilities, physical network safeguards, and locking of software distribution media.

3. Handling encryption and encrypted data:

   - Policies on when to encrypt data can specify that data could be classified based on storage or transmission requirements. Data classified in certain areas would then be encrypted.

   - Exceptions can be made, especially for backup media, that would have a difficult key management and recovery procedure.

   - After data is encrypted, policies can mandate that data is thoroughly deleted or the media is destroyed to prevent it from being accessible by anyone.

4. Key generation considerations:

   - One of the most important aspects of dealing with encryption is the *key*. In encryption, the key is the variable applied to the algorithm to encrypt the data. The key is usually a secret value or has a secret component. It is important to ensure that the key remains a secret.

   - Policies can specify certain rules that should be followed, leaving it up to the administrators to create the appropriate process.

   - Key generation policies can cover allowable formats, storage requirements, expiration issues, and the privacy of the key generation software and procedures.

   - Policies can mandate the destruction of key generating materials by specifying overwriting of memory and online storage. Other policies can call for the destruction of external storage materials.

5. Key management:

- Key management is difficult because of the differences between types of encryption and the standards that apply to different mechanisms.

- Regardless of the type of encryption used, keys will have to be disclosed at some point. Disclosure requirements can be governed through service agreements or by the requirements of the software or devices used. Policies can be written to cover how keys are disclosed as well as the management of key recovery or key escrow systems.

- Certain aspects of key storage cannot be controlled. Key storage policies can cover how keys are stored, backed up, or stored for transmission. One area that always seems to be a concern is the storage of keys on the same device or media as the protected data.

- Key transmission issues differ with the type of algorithms used and whether encrypted transmission services are outsourced. Public key or asymmetric technologies have fewer concerns because the public key can be transmitted openly without worrying about compromise. Those using symmetric encryption must find alternatives. A general policy can be written to mandate an out-of-band transmission without specifying how that will occur.

10

Software Development Policies

SOFTWARE DEVELOPMENT IS THE ART OF putting together coded instructions in a manner that will be translated into a meaningful program to run on a computer. Like other arts based on scientific theories, mistakes and other flaws can lead to catastrophic results. With the explosion of the Internet, flaws in the software that serve web pages, transmit email, or provide access to other servers have made systems vulnerable to attack.

Software development methodologies have rarely considered security as a component of design. Often, security becomes an afterthought causing unusual measures to be employed. By including software development within security policies, organizations can prevent ad hoc redevelopment, thus keeping their in-house development from creating security vulnerabilities. This chapter discusses the software development process and how it influences organizational security that includes development, testing, and configuration management. Even if your organization does not develop its own software, there are aspects of these policies, such as configuration management and third-party development, that might be appropriate.

Scope of Software Development Policies

When writing a book that will be marketed to a relatively general audience, it is difficult to write about specific problems faced by organizations of different sizes. Rather than explore every possibility, this chapter discusses policies as if an organization has a staff doing software development. The size of this staff is not an issue, and I leave it to the reader to make appropriate adjustments to my suggestions to fit his or her environment.

Software Development Processes

As much as anyone would like to pontificate on the software development process, information security policies should stay away from this debate. If your organization has software development policies and procedures, the developers might loathe having their processes changed. Otherwise, this can be the catalyst to develop procedures. In either case, the place where information security policies fits into the software development process is in augmenting their efforts and ensuring that security is considered during design and development.

Identifying Software Development Responsibilities

Security policies for software development should identify where the responsibilities lie in promoting secure development and deployment of software. Just like the issues of ownership that were discussed in Chapter 2, "Determining Your Policy Needs," assignment of responsibilities can make people accountable for developing or acquiring secure solutions. Policies in this area also should mandate that security requirements be identified prior to development or the acquisition of software. This can be written as follows:

> *All software development and acquisition requirements shall include security requirements consistent with these policies. The author of the overall requirements shall be responsible for ensuring that security requirements are specified.*

Now that the policy is written to require security in development, some organizations feel that adding a policy statement directed at the programmers is necessary. A technical manager once said that many of his young, talented programmers do not understand the ramifications of these requirements and will look for ways to program around them. By making it a requirement through the policy, it reinforces their compliance. That manager suggested the following policy statement:

> *All programmers involved in development and maintenance shall subscribe to all policies, standards, procedures, and other development conventions.*

Establishing Software Development Policies

One time I sat with a client and started to talk about security and software development policies, and I received blank looks in return. I asked if the organization had any type of policies or standards for software development. The director, whose responsibility was in-house development, sheepishly said that they did but that the employees did not follow them.

After some discussion, we decided to develop a framework for maintaining security throughout the software development lifecycle while promoting established standards and policies. By using the compliance requirements of the information security policies with the backing of management on all levels, they felt that developers would be compelled to follow these rules. Some might see this as using the security policies to change the culture of the organization. However, those managers in this situation could see it as an opening to make changes for the better.

To help this client, I took the stand that there are three basic rules that can promote the development of secure software as well as the software development policy. They can be considered fundamental rules of software development. By including them as part of the information security policy, you can create a new focus on these rules. Translating these rules into policy statements, they can say

> No software development shall occur without formal specifications. These specifications shall include requirements for security and privacy of the data being collected and processed.

> All software shall verify and acknowledge user input, regardless of outcome.

> All software shall check and verify boundaries of data transferred to and from blocks of memory to prevent overwriting of critical data and programs.

The last two statements address the buffer overflow problem, which is perceived as the most common problem in software security. It seems that a large number of problems occur because programmers either forget to include bounds checking or assume that it cannot occur in that circumstance. In either case, by including them in the policy you can focus on the potential problem and force mitigation before something happens.

Access Controls in Software

Other problems that affect the security of custom software are the trap doors or special access controls developers give to themselves under the guise of debugging or being able to maintain the software. These access paths are usually not documented and go unnoticed until something goes wrong. One organization discovered that one former employee used such a "backdoor" to download proprietary data that was sold to competitors. The losses to this organization included the cost of hiring an outside consultant to audit and remove other access paths.

Adding to my basic rules of secure software development, there are two more statements that should help prevent these problems. Although they are similar, they are written to cover all access paths that will bypass security regardless of the reason they were added. These policy statements can say

> No software shall be installed or considered for installation that includes shortcuts, trap doors, or any path that may circumvent security.

> No software shall be installed or considered for installation that includes special access privileges for developers.

Access Policies and HIPAA

Those reading this in the healthcare industry might see the conflict with certain provisions of the Health Insurance Portability and Accountability Act (HIPAA) . Although HIPAA attempts to improve the security and privacy of personal data maintained by healthcare providers, it also has a provision that allows practitioners to gain access to a patient's clinical information without requiring authorization or authentication. The purpose of this built-in backdoor or shortcut required by HIPAA is to ensure critical data is made available to healthcare providers in the event of an emergency.

Although HIPAA does not clarify how to write policies and procedures for emergency situations, healthcare organizations should consider looking beyond HIPAA and consider a balance between being able to provide timely healthcare and the privacy of this personal data in their policies.

The next policy statement should address who is responsible for access control and security. Under the policy, the controls should be given to the administrators or the owners of the processes and data. To do that, not only do controls have to be designed into the package from the beginning of the development cycle, but it also has to conform to the standards used by your organization. Simply write a statement that requires software developers to comply with established standards:

> *All access privileges and controls built into custom software shall conform to the standard administrative controls as outlined by these policies and associated guidelines.*

Other Policy Considerations

For the most part, this section has covered enough policy issues to ensure that there is a basis for secure software development. However, some organizations feel that additional policies are required in order to use the security policies to further strengthen their software development efforts.

One manager of a mainframe shop was concerned about the proliferation of microcomputers and their new programming language. During the policy-writing process, he convinced the committee to include a statement that read

> *All software development shall use one programming language consistent across projects.*

Another organization was trying to migrate from the mainframe to servers and microcomputers. Their managers were concerned about developing secure software and being able to reuse it across projects. Rather than making it specific to security issues, they wrote a statement that addressed all reusability concerns. Their statement was similar to this:

> *All software development shall consider reusing components of other projects.*
> *Software development shall consider reusability a secondary goal of the project.*

The growth of open software is a cause of concern for some managers. These managers worry that these tools are not mature enough to prevent some of the classic development problems, such as buffer overflows. One organization that had this concern wrote a policy statement that said

All software development shall only use mature development tools and techniques.

Finally, one organization was worried that installed software would become too intertwined with the system name space and that it would be impossible to identify and fix problems. Although this caused an argument among the committee, they compromised and included a statement that read

All software development shall use a single naming convention for all production files.

The problem with software development policies is that they can arouse fervent debate. Although it is possible to include anything in the policies, I would suggest that you reconsider adding items that may be best left to procedures.

Authentication Design Rules

A large amount of software is designed to support business functions that should be limited to specific users. Although this is not always the case, much of the software developed might include requirements that the user be identified and authorized to access these functions. Identification and authorization (I&A) are fundamental security mechanisms to guard the front door into the program. Because of their importance, most organizations look for policies to shore up their development policies to ensure I&A is properly handled.

A director of development noted that when he arrived at the organization, the many projects they supported used several different mechanisms to provide I&A functions. Some of them were even incompatible with the operating system, database, or other mechanisms that controlled major software systems. The remedy is to try to use a common mechanism that is integrated with the system or database. Aside from being easier to manage, it uses currently available and mature security mechanisms to protect both the custom development and the system or database. This director suggested a policy statement that said

Identification and Authorization of custom developed software shall use and integrate the mechanisms of the operating system, database, or supporting software system in its design and deployment.

Other policies involving the I&A process concern themselves with the handling of the password information. Although some of these policies have been called a common-sense approach to developing I&A, many have realized that they can be forgotten as part of the development process. Therefore, it might be best to include them in your policies. Some of the possible policies include

Passwords shall not be sent via electronic mail without being encrypted.

Passwords shall not be transmitted in clear text across the network without having been encrypted.

Passwords shall not be stored in clear text on accessible storage devices.

Passwords shall never be a static value stored within the program (hard-coded).

Memory used for deciphering and checking passwords shall be cleared once processing is completed.

Testing and Documentation

One of the most neglected areas of software development security policies is the area of testing and documentation. Both are important components of software development, but they have security implications. A comprehensive testing plan can help find a number of problems before they go into production. However, proper documentation can assist testers in understanding what is being tested. Therefore, these policies should start with the requirement for testing and documentation. A simple statement can say

All custom development shall be tested and documented before being installed into the production environment.

It is important to note that this statement is establishing the requirement, not the type of testing or format of the documentation. This is an exercise that should be included as part of the overall software policies and procedures.

Generating Test Data

During a consulting assignment many years ago, I started to work with the group responsible for testing the software I wrote. While the testers were demonstrating certain problems, I noticed that the data being used included personal information of well-known clients of this organization. After seeing several familiar names, I asked where they made up this data. The test team admitted that they extracted real data from the organization's database to create test data.

I was very surprised. The data contained personal information of famous people that had never been publicly disclosed. Additionally, it was evident that the test team had read the data based on their not-so-flattering comments. Later, when I became more involved with information security and policy writing, I was insistent on including policies that protected sensitive data from this type of disclosure.

Over time, I have heard a number of arguments for using real data for testing. The most compelling is that it is an accurate representation of what these programs must process. After I relay my story, I ask them how they plan to safeguard the personal or proprietary information of clients. After much thought, most agree that some safeguards are necessary. When the debates settle, most agree to a policy that is similar to the following:

> *Data used to test software shall be generated from production data to properly simulate real situations. This data shall be sanitized to remove sensitive or proprietary information prior to its use.*

Testing and Acceptance

The test procedure should be designed to ferret out all possible problems and security violations. If the software passes the testing phase, it should be accepted and installed in the production environment. While these procedures are out of the scope of information security policies, certain aspects of this process can be subjects of policy. In the context of information security, we look to prevent a denial of service based on the problems that could occur when installing software with bugs or unexpected side effects.

When testing has successfully completed, the policies should mandate that a plan be created to install the new software. It does not matter if the software is an upgrade or new development; the plan should include notifying users, operating documentation, and a way to reverse the installation should something go wrong. This can be written in three short policy statements:

> *Software accepted from testing shall include a plan to install it into the production environment. This plan shall include procedures for uninstalling the software should it become necessary.*

> *Installation shall not occur without notifying users to the procedures and error-reporting requirements.*

> *Software accepted for installation shall not be installed without appropriate operating documentation.*

Documentation Requirements

Documentation is not a requirement of secure systems. It is necessary for understanding how to use the system and how it works. This documentation helps future developers understand the interfaces and how these interfaces are supposed to function. They ultimately disclose the workings of the software system that can be used to analyze whether there are problems or side effects that can impact information security.

Documentation should not be limited to the use of the system. Along with the requirements, developers should document the design, each component, and their interfaces. This will prevent the duplication of efforts as well as document the controls programmed into the software that meet the security requirements. The policy to express this desire can say

> *Software development procedures shall include user and technical documentation that describes how the software works; how it is operated; its inputs and outputs; interfaces with the system and other components; and the security controls it uses.*

Revision Control and Configuration Management

As a followup to testing and acceptance policies in the previous sections, one way to ensure the ability to uninstall versions of software is through *revision control* or *configuration management*. The security impact of change management is knowing the configuration of the system and its components. By knowing what is supposed to be in the system and the network, the administrators can tell if security has been violated and rogue programs have been installed on the system.

Some aspects of configuration management duplicate the policies that were discussed for software development. However, not everything under this system will be from software development. They are included here to amplify their importance for the software development process as well as to ensure the safe installation of operating system and even off-the-shelf components. The processes that require notice in security policies are the procedures to request the change, require testing, and installation procedures. You can establish this program with the following statement:

> *A configuration management program shall be established to maintain the configuration of all production systems, including operating systems, off-the-shelf software, and security controls.*

Revision Control Request Procedures

One of the key security aspects of revision control and configuration management is the ability to track changes. If problems occur, administrators can examine the system in the context of the software and other installed components to see what may have caused the problem. The first step in creating these traces is to have a policy that mandates a formal change control procedure for all production systems. This policy provides for written requests to perform system changes that can include a review for security:

> *Revision control and configuration management shall establish a formal change control procedure for all production systems. These procedures shall include mechanisms for written change requests, maintaining the sources of development software installed on production systems, and a review of security controls.*

The policy does not mandate a specific way of performing this work nor the software that could be used in the process. Once again, leave this as an implementation detail.

Configuration Management and Security Fixes

It can be considered inevitable that installed software will have bugs. Some of these bugs can be an inconvenience in operations. Others will have security implications. It has been a source of debate among security and systems administration professionals as to how to handle fixing the software that has security problems. On one hand, there is the need to fix the problem immediately to prevent problems. However, installing patches, even from a vendor, can lead to unpredicted results.

Large organizations have the ability to create test systems in order to test these changes before installing them into the production environment. Smaller organizations might not have this luxury and must patch production systems. In either case, either organization can leave these details to the procedures and write a policy to cover these situations. To accomplish this, your policy statement can say

> *Configuration management shall have procedures in place to test and install security fixes from developers and vendors.*

Configuration Management and Maintenance

Late one day while working with a client on these policies, a manager turned to me and asked how to write a policy that would force programmers to port their patches to the program's source after they patched the object deck. This was a mainframe shop whose cavalier programmers would test and patch the binary of the software without patching the source code. When other problems occurred, the developers would forget about patching the binary, and old problems returned when they applied the next fix to the source.

This is not a problem in many organizations because this type of work requires a lot of experience. Although it is more common for this to happen in a mainframe environment, there is nothing to prevent it from occurring elsewhere. To prevent it from happening in your organization, a simple policy can help. Try the following:

> *All maintenance on custom developed software shall be performed on the program's source and not its associated binary.*

Testing Before Installation

One of the dangers of working in change management is allowing the installation of software before it is tested. Testing will be able to determine that the software can interoperate in the environment and does not open any new security problems. There will be a temptation to load patches without testing, especially vendor-supplied secu-rity patches.

Policy should require the testing and accepting of these patches whether a vendor or the in-house development staff supplies them. The policy does not have to specify the testing be performed on specific systems, but it should set the parameters. This will allow organizations with fewer resources to devise a plan that will fit its environment. A good generic policy statement could read

> *All software shall undergo testing and acceptance prior to using in a production environment. This policy shall include vendor-supplied software and patches as well as those developed in-house.*

Installation Procedures

Regardless of how much software is tested, there will be a case when installed software or patches must be uninstalled from the production environment. For that reason, con-figuration management policies should include the requirement to have both installa-tion and the ability to recover from an installation. A statement can read

> *Configuration management procedures shall include procedures to install and roll-back to a previous version should problems occur.*

Third-Party Development

Some organizations do not have the expertise necessary to do some custom software development. In recent times, it is common for organizations to hire companies to do web development. These and other third-party development projects represent poten-tial security hazards that could expose your organization to problems. The policies you develop for third-party development should be designed to protect your organization.

Policy to Guarantee Integrity

When an organization outsources its software development, there has to be a concern over the integrity of the software that is the result of that development. How is the organization sure that this software will not contain undocumented features, backdoors, or other mechanisms to circumvent security? Policies in this area are similar to those for software development. The difference is that these policies are directed to the third party and the agreements forming those relationships. This policy can say

> *All agreements with third-party software developers shall include a statement of integrity. This statement shall include assurances of no undocumented features and that the software developed shall not include backdoors, trapdoors, or other mecha-nisms to circumvent security.*

Statement of integrity can go one step further, especially if the developed software will run on the organization's systems and network. In addition to ensuring that the software does what it is supposed to do, it should be able to work with the security controls of the operating environment on which it will be installed. By not following established guidelines and mechanisms, the software could wind up violating security policies. Therefore, to extend the integrity policy, a policy statement can be added that says

> *All third-party developed software shall comply with established information security standards. This software shall be able to be integrated with the controls of operating system or management software.*

Restriction Commercial Distribution

When an organization uses a third-party developer to create custom software, that third party will have programmed in a certain amount of business intelligence so that it works to your organization's specifications. The third party might see value in the processes and consider packaging the software your organization paid to develop to be sold on the open market. Although this would be flattering, the third party also might be selling your business processes to your competitors.

In the modern world of web development, the third-party designers are relying on software packages that they developed as the basis of the services they offer. In this environment, there can be fewer restrictions on the redistribution of development. In fact, your organization might have no control over the third party. This doubt should be considered for your policy. One way of writing the policy can be

> *Where possible, third parties developing software for the organization shall not sell or redistribute this software. Documentation associated with this software shall not be distributed.*

Escrow for Third-Party Software

I was once working for a manufacturer of telecommunications equipment programming embedded systems. One day, my boss asked me to create a set of PROMs (programmable read-only memory, special memory circuits whose data usually cannot be erased). He then wanted me to print out the source of the programs stored on those PROMs and give them to someone who would place them in escrow. I became curious and asked why we were doing this. I was told it was the request of the client, who worried about what would happen should the company go out of business.

Less than a year later, the company started to lose money and was closed a short time thereafter. I do not know if the client ever used the information stored in the escrow, but it was there even though the company was out of business.

As the number of recent failures of Internet software companies has increased, your organization may want to consider what would happen if the company that is developing your web site goes out of business. In most cases, when these companies close their doors, obtaining any of their assets is difficult. However, if your organization has the third party place copies of the software (including the source) in escrow, your organization could either maintain the software using in-house developers, or you could give this information to another third party to maintain.

The following policy statement was borrowed from a client who was a web developer. By offering agreements to place a copy of their software in escrow, they seemed to garner more respect from the business community. They provided this statement after negotiating a few of these agreements:

> *All third-party development agreements shall include a provision to place a copy of the source and executable programs into escrow. These provisions shall allow the organization to access that escrow should the third party fail to maintain the software.*

Intellectual Property Issues

Regardless of who performs the development, the final result can be considered intellectual property. This intellectual property contains the business process and other proprietary information as to how the organization operates on a daily basis. These programs should be treated as valuable assets.

In the context of information security, gaining knowledge of this intellectual property can give an outsider a view of the internal workings of the organization. This knowledge can provide guides to actual or social engineering of the systems and the people using the systems. The result could be electronic break-ins or other computer security problems that could be masked by using this internal knowledge.

Most organizations have an intellectual property policy that is separate from the information security policies. These policies are usually written by attorneys to protect intellectual property regardless of its intended use. If your organization has such a policy, you should not include it within the security policy. Rather, a paragraph should be made within the Acceptable Use Policy (see Chapter 11, "Acceptable Use Policies") to inform the user of the existence of such a policy.

For those organizations without an intellectual property policy, it might be worth the resources to ensure your organization creates one. Because these policies must comply with the appropriate laws, which can be complex, your organization should employ an attorney whose specialty is intellectual property to help with this endeavor. It is really beyond the scope of an information security policy.

Summary

Software development is the art of putting together coded instructions in a manner that will be translated into meaningful programs that run on a computer. Like other arts based on scientific theories, mistakes and other flaws can lead to catastrophic results. Often, security becomes an afterthought, causing unusual measures to be employed. By including software development within security policies, organizations can prevent ad hoc redevelopment, thus, keeping their in-house development from creating security vulnerabilities. Even if your organization does not develop its own software, there are aspects of these policies that might be appropriate.

1. Software development processes:

   - Software development policies help ensure that security is considered during design and development.

   - Security policies for software development should identify where the responsibilities lie in promoting secure development and deployment of software.

   - Establishing software development policies can be based on three basic rules that can promote the development of secure software as well as the software development policy: require specifications, verify and acknowledge user input, and check and verify boundaries of data during transfers.

   - Adding to these basic rules of secure software development, there are two policies that should help prevent security problems: no trap doors or any other mechanism that may circumvent security and the removal of special access privileges for developers.

   - Establish that access controls built into custom software conform to standard practices and guidelines.

   - Policies for identification and authorization of custom developed software should be integrated into the mechanisms of the operating system, database, or supporting software system in its design and deployment.

   - Other policies involving the identification and authorization process concern themselves with the handling of the password information.

2. Testing and documentation:

   - One of the most neglected areas of software development security policies is the area of testing and documentation. Both are important components of software development, but they have security implications.

   - A policy should be included to safeguard the personal or proprietary information of clients by restricting the use of this data during software testing.

   - The test procedure should be designed to ferret out all possible problems and security violations. Policies can be written to prevent software from being installed if it does not pass testing and acceptance.

   - Documentation is not a requirement of secure systems. It helps future developers understand the interfaces and how these interfaces are supposed to function by ultimately disclosing the workings of the software system that can be used to analyze whether there are problems or side effects that can impact information security.

3. Revision control and configuration management:

   - The security impact of change management is to provide a blueprint of the system and its components. By knowing what is supposed to be installed on the system and the network, the administrators can tell if security has been violated and rogue programs have been installed on the system.

   - One of the key security aspects of revision control and configuration management is the ability to track changes. This policy provides for written requests to perform system changes that can include a review for security.

   - It can be considered inevitable that installed software will have bugs. There will always be a need to fix the problems immediately to prevent further problems. However, installing patches, even from a vendor, can lead to unpredicted results. Policies in this area should mandate that procedures be in place to test and install security fixes prior to installation.

   - Regardless of how much software is tested, there will be a case when installed software or patches must be uninstalled from the production environment. Configuration management policies should include the requirement to have both installation and the ability to recover from an installation.

4. Third-party development:

   - Some organizations do not have the expertise necessary to do some custom software development. Third-party development projects represent potential security hazards that could expose your organization to problems.

   - When an organization outsources its software development, there has to be a concern over the integrity of the software that results from that development. Policies in this area are similar to those for software development except that these policies are directed to the third party and the agreements forming those relationships.

   - In addition to ensuring that the software does what it is supposed to do, it should be able to work with the security controls of the operating environment on which it will be installed. By not following established guidelines and mechanisms, the software could wind up violating security policies.

   - When an organization uses a third-party developer to create custom software, they might see value in the processes and consider packaging the software your organization paid to develop to be sold on the open market. Although this can be flattering, the third party also might be selling your business processes to your competitors. Policies can be written to mandate that agreements contain sale and distribution clauses.

- As the dot-com boom turns to bust yet again, your organization might want to consider what would happen if the company that is developing your web site goes out of business. In most cases, when these companies close their doors, obtaining any of their assets will be difficult. If your organization had the third party place a copy of the software (including the source) in escrow, the organization could either maintain the software in-house, or you will be able to give this information to another developer to maintain.

5. Intellectual property issues:

- Regardless of who does the development, the final result can be considered intellectual property of the organization. This intellectual property contains the business process and other proprietary information as to how the organization operates. These programs should be treated as valuable assets to the organization.

- For those organizations without an intellectual property policy, it might be worth the resources to ensure your organization creates one. Because these policies must comply with the appropriate laws, which can be complex, your organization should employ an attorney whose specialty is intellectual property to help with this endeavor.

Maintaining the Policies

11

Acceptable Use Policies

IF YOU HAVE FOLLOWED THE OUTLINE OF THIS book, you should have completed most of the work on your organization's information security policies. With the bulk of the work completed, you can turn your attention to a summarized version called an *Acceptable Use Policy* (AUP).

An AUP is a document that summarizes the overall policy for the users. The AUP can contain parts of the organization's policies outlining the user's security responsibilities. Most of the time, they are highlighted components and written in plain language. A successful AUP is short and to the point. Ideally, the AUP should only be a few pages.

Usually, the AUP is a signed document that acts as an agreement to abide by the information security policies it represents. It can be given to the new employee, contractor, or vendor with access to the network to ensure they know their responsibilities. The purpose is to draw attention to the policy documents without requiring the new user to read them. Sure the AUP should say that the user will abide by the policies, but AUP can be seen as a "quick start" document to allow users to read the full policy later.

Sample AUP
Although this chapter will include sample statements, Appendix C, "Sample Policies," includes a sample AUP.

Writing the AUP

Although the AUP is an important document, it should be short and to the point. One of the problems that you might face when writing the AUP is that you are now treading on the turf of different organizations. The organization's Human Resources Department will want to ensure that the policy complies with both the organization's hiring policies and the various labor laws with which they also must comply. Then there are those who negotiate with contractor and vendors who must include the AUP and the policies in the contract with those third parties.

As easy as the AUP sounds, some organizations find that it is the most difficult document to write. In one organization, the discussion table turned into a war-room mentality when Management, Human Resources, a department that used a lot of contractors, and the attorneys sat to try to finalize the AUP. For this group, it took three meetings and several interim emails to come to a consensus.

The Language of the AUP

Throughout this book, I have used a very formal language in the sample policy statements (see the sidebar, "The Language of Policy Documents," in Chapter 4, "Physical Security"). Just as language can represent the organization for the policy documents, it can do the same for the AUP. Because the AUP is usually the first document someone reads, I prefer to use a plain and somewhat informational language style in the AUP.

You have to be careful with language you use. If you are not, you can send the wrong message. If the language is too informal or too wordy, the AUP might not be taken seriously. If the language is too formal, users might not take the policy seriously. The key is to strike the right balance.

Generally, the AUP should be simple and simply organized. So when I help organizations write their AUP documents, I like to see them organize it in the following manner:

- *Introduction and Purpose.* Start with a paragraph explaining what the AUP is, its purpose, and the policies on which it is based. Some organizations, at the request of their attorneys, add a statement of scope saying what areas the policies cover.
- *Recognize a "Higher Authority."* The AUP is based on the policies that were just completed. Add a statement that recognizes this and where the user can see a copy of the policies. Also let the user know that the policy can change. You can include a statement such as

    > *This Acceptable User Policy is based on the organization's Information Security Policies. Copies of the Information Security Policies are available from the administrative assistant for each department or electronically on the organization's intranet.*

    > *These policies are subject to change. The organization may elect to change these policies without prior notice. If changes are made, users will be notified via electronic mail.*

- *Term.* I was surprised to learn that legal documents of the type you are developing require a statement defining the duration that they are in force. A good generic statement can read

  > *The user agrees to abide by this Acceptable User Policy and the Information Security Policy effective from the date signed until the user terminates their association with the organization.*

- *User Responsibilities.* Because the AUP is a summary, it could include highlights from the policies that should be emphasized. The rest of this chapter will discuss some provisions that might be included in the AUP.

User Login Responsibilities

After starting the AUP with legalities and required components, it might be nice to discuss something less daunting, like user login responsibilities. This section is nothing more than a summary of the authentication policy (see Chapter 5, "Authentication and Network Security"). Here, the user highlights are covered—the items they should know even if they have not read the entire policy document.

One simple method to get the point across is to prepare a bulleted list of short statements to include in the AUP. Those items could say

- *You will be required to enter your username and password in order to log in to the network.*

- *If you enter your password incorrectly three times in a row, your account will be locked and you will not be able to log in until it is unlocked by an administrator.*

- *Passwords will be changed every 60 days. You will be reminded to change your password three days in advance. If you do not change your password by the end of the 60 days, your account will be locked and you will not be able to log in until an administrator unlocks it.*

- *You should never write down your password.*

- *You are responsible for protecting your user identification and password. If you suspect someone else knows your password, you must change it immediately and report it to the administrator.*

- *You must not share your user identification and password with anyone. If there is a requirement to grant access to an outside user, that user must follow appropriate procedures to apply for access.*

- *If you forget your password or must have it reset by the administrator, you must do it in person.*

Use of Systems and Network

Now that the user can log in, the next thing he or she needs to know is what can and cannot be done on the network. In this section you reiterate many areas of the policy that cover daily use. These are the rules of general conduct as outlined by the policies. Some of the provisions you can include are

- *Systems and network are to be used for business purposes only. Incidental personal use is permitted as long as it is not more than a trivial amount of time and does not interfere with your tasks.*

- *The organization's connectivity to the Internet is to be treated as a business resource. The same usage rules apply as above.*

- *Users must not use the systems, network, or Internet connection to play games.*

- *The organization maintains a standard configuration for all systems. Users will not install non-standard software without prior authorization.*

- *Users are reminded that organizational information is proprietary and may not be shared with any outsider. You can copy this information as necessary to complete your task. You also may share this information only with appropriate personnel.*

- *If you have to share proprietary information with outside users, you should consult with the policies as to how this can be done safely.*

User Responsibilities

Chapter 6, "Internet Security Policies," included a section within the Internet Policy that outlined user responsibilities. These policies are intended to be a code of conduct for those using the Internet connection. We include a separate section for Internet users to recognize the growing importance of the Internet as a resource and the special nature of communications caused by its openness.

When writing the AUP, you should consider including policies that are unique to using the Internet and not items included in the general systems and network policy. Remember, our goal is to keep the AUP short and to the point. To do this you should try not to repeat policy statements.

Therefore, we should try to prioritize the most important aspects of the Internet policy and include them as summary statements in the AUP. Considering the discussion in Chapter 6, there are four areas that you might want to cover in the AUP. Sample statements covering these issues are as follows:

- *Every message and request sent to the Internet includes information that associates you with our organization. Therefore, users will conduct themselves in a professional manner and should not access sites that promote illegal, sexual, or other information that would be inconsistent with policies.*

- *Users are reminded that Internet communications are not private. When online, users must be careful as to what they disclose to others. Users should refrain from sending out any information that may be damaging to the organization or themselves.*

- *Users will not transmit any information that discloses the intellectual property of business intelligence of the organization. This includes sending documents or other data to people outside of the organization without taking appropriate precautions.*

- *Users who download software from the Internet will do so on systems protected by up-to-date anti-virus software. The anti-virus software must be operating while downloaded software is running on the user's system. If the installation of the software requires the disabling of the anti-virus software, the user must perform a complete anti-virus scan of the system after the installation is completed.*

Finally, if a training program is part of your Internet policy, include a simple statement in the AUP that could say

Users wishing to access the Internet must first complete a training course.

Organization's Responsibilities and Disclosures

The users are not the only ones with responsibilities according to your information security policies. The organization has a responsibility to let its users know what the policy says they are required to do and what it is going to do. Aside from being responsible, the organization has a legal obligation to disclose what they are doing, such as monitoring and collecting data crossing their network. Without the required disclosures, the courts have discounted data collected and policy violations by users.

Sometimes these policies are difficult to add to the AUP. There have been reports that users have looked upon these statements in a negative light. This has lead to an adversarial relationship between management and those who directly enforce the policy—it has changed some organizations' cultures. The key is to write policy statements that say exactly what the organization is going to do under the policy and ensure that it does not imply something harsher.

Monitoring and Examination of Network Data

The area in which organizations get into the most trouble is when they do not disclose that they are monitoring the network and files stored on the organization's systems. This usually happens after an administrator finds something objectionable on a server or transmitted on the network that leads to some type of disciplinary action. If the user decides to take legal action and the courts find that the organization did not disclose its monitoring policies, the court will rule against the organization.

Whenever there has been a question whether or not to disclose, attorneys have said to err on the side of caution and add it to the AUP. Unfortunately, there is not a good way of saying that the organization is allowed to play "big brother" while the users are using the network. Sometimes it might be necessary to just provide a blunt statement so there is no confusion. Here is a sample blunt statement showing the extreme policy statement:

> *Management reserves the right to examine data stored on all computer and network systems through both physical examination and electronic monitoring. If the information collected reveals violations to the information security policies or the law, the organization may use its discoveries for disciplinary actions or provide them to law enforcement.*

Collection of Private Data

If the organization is monitoring data, it is more than likely that some of that data is being collected. Even if the organization is not actively monitoring its network, there are other information sources from which the organization might collect records. Regardless, if information is being collected, the organization should say what they are collecting, how it is collected, and how it is stored.

This is not an easy topic for some organizations because this could put the AUP at odds with human resource policy. The AUP and the process could be seen as circumventing Human Resources and could cause hard feelings. It is best to work with Human Resources to help define what should be in the AUP and what should be reserved for Human Resources. Regardless, there are a few things that should be considered for policy statements. The following is a short, non-exclusive list of things to include:

- Disclose information that could be collected from users.
- Organization may state that they will not collect information about users' expression of first amendment rights.
- The need to collect private information must first be justified.
- The organization understands that when private data is collected, its distribution is prohibited.
- It should be stated if and what kind of performance monitoring is allowed.
- The policy should guarantee the privacy of collected data that is allowed to be collected unless disclosure is required by a court order.
- One from the attorneys: You can include a disclaimer of responsibility that says the organization can exercise its authority without notice and disclaims responsibility for loss or damage to data and software as a result.

Common-Sense Guidelines About Speech

While helping an organization write its information security policies, some in a committee they gathered saw the concept of adding speech guidelines to the AUP as "caving in to the evils of political correctness." This organization's culture was very informal. Management prided themselves on being treated the same as the lowest employee. They did not want to be viewed as the corporate "big brother" and break that team and family feeling.

A few days after these discussions, the newspapers printed a front-page news story about a harassment and discrimination lawsuit being filed against a major oil company. Allegedly, an executive was accused of discrimination against subordinates. To prove their case, the employees used archived email sent by the executive. The company eventually apologized publicly and said the executive exercised poor judgment.

This news story had an impact. At our next meeting the Vice President that was sponsoring the writing of their information security policies slid a paper across the table to me. It read

> While we [sic] like to think of ourselves as a family, as a member of this family you have to remember that we are all individuals who may not see things the same as you. This means that you should consider how that person might feel when you talk about politics, religion, or use language some may consider foul. Aside from not being proper family values, it is against the law to say or write anything that could be considered harassing to another person whether the comment is about their race, age, sex, physical nature, or sexual orientation. If you cannot accept and follow these values, you will be asked to leave our family and will be terminated.

I made some minor adjustments and included this statement in their AUP.

Summary

An Acceptable Use Policy (AUP) is a document that summarizes the overall policy for the users. The AUP can contain parts of the organization's policies outlining the user's security responsibilities. Most of the time, they are highlighted components and written in plain language. Usually, the AUP is a short document that can be used as an agreement to abide by the information security policies. It can be given to the new employee, contractor, or vendor with access to the network to ensure they know their responsibilities.

1. Writing the AUP:
   - The AUP is an important document. It should be short and to the point. One of the problems you might face when writing the AUP is that you might have to coordinate different departments to complete the document.
   - Generally, the AUP should be simple and simply organized.
2. User login responsibilities:
   - This section should be a summary of the authentication policy (see Chapter 5).
   - Users are presented with the highlights of the items they should know even if they have not read the entire policy document.

3. Use of systems and network:
   - This section reiterates the many areas of the policy that cover daily use.
   - They are the rules of general conduct as outlined within the different policies.
4. Internet user responsibilities:
   - Internet policies outline user responsibilities. These policies were intended to be a code of conduct for those using the Internet connection. We include a separate section for Internet users to recognize the growing importance of the Internet as a resource but also the special nature of communication.
   - The AUP should include polices that are unique to using the Internet.
   - Prioritize the most important aspects of the Internet policy and include them as summary statements in the AUP.
5. Organization's responsibilities and disclosures:
   - The organization has a responsibility to let its users know what the policy says they are required to do and what it is going to do. There might be a legal obligation to disclose what they are doing, such as monitoring and collecting data crossing its network.
   - Whenever the policies allow monitoring of network transmission or user files, the AUP should disclose these facts.
   - The organization should disclose if it is collecting information on its users from any source. The policy might include statements of how that data is collected and what is stored. The key is disclosure, which could prevent problems if that information is used for any type of disciplinary action.
6. Common-sense guidelines about speech:
   - You can add a statement of guidelines about speech that will help prevent certain problems in the future. These guidelines were discussed in previous chapters.
   - Some organizations find it easier to use an informal style to get the point across. The key is to get the point across in a way that users will pay attention.

12

Compliance and Enforcement

AFTER THE INFORMATION SECURITY POLICIES FOR the systems and networks have been written, your focus should switch to what it would take to ensure compliance and enforce the policy. It would be nice if we could trust the users and anyone with access to the organization's network. To ensure the systems and networks are protected, you should define compliance and enforcement policies that explain what could happen when policy is broken.

Compliance and enforcement policies tend to fall outside of the technical arena that most security professionals live. By their nature, these policies require knowledge of various corporate policies as well as compliance to various laws, including intellectual property, labor, and possibly criminal law. Thus, it is important that a representative for all affected areas be present while discussing these policies.

On the Advice of Counsel...
Throughout this book I have given examples of policy statements for you to use as guidelines when writing your policy. You may have adopted those samples in the policies you are writing. Please remember that the samples have been taken from my experiences and those requiring legal interpretation are from the appropriate jurisdiction. Therefore, I highly recommend that your organization consult the appropriate counsel to verify that the statements are legal where your company is located.

Testing and Effectiveness of the Policies

This section is sometimes called the *Policies of the Policy*. It is where you set the parameters, starting with the basics of how to measure the performance of the policies. We are not talking about testing the mechanisms, but how the policies are impacted by business requirements through compliance mechanisms.

Testing compliance is a very subjective process. Most of the organizations I have worked with like to keep statistics on violations and waivers granted. The net result is to have information that can be used when reevaluating information security policies. Therefore, the policies you write in this section will cover the notification and report processes with your measurements. Also, as amplification, I would include a policy statement on security awareness training.

Starting with security awareness training, after the policies are written there must be communication between the writers, management, and everyone in the organization to understand the policies and their impact. Management should not only set aside time, but encourage this training. By making training the first policy statement of this section, you are saying that training is a very important component of this security plan. This can be captured in a statement that says

> All users of the organization's network and systems shall undergo security-awareness training to explain these security policies prior to being allowed access. Current users shall undergo training within 30 days from when these policies are put into place.

After making the users aware of the information security policies, the next step is to demonstrate measures of compliance. These measures can be used to test the effectiveness. Remember, these are policies, so you do not want to get into specifics as to how to go about this. The policies can specify that administrators maintain statistics and other information on security violations as well as waivers that might have been granted. Thus a policy can be included to say

> Security, Systems, and Network Administrators shall maintain records of all security violations. These records shall be in sufficient detail so that they may be used for disciplinary actions and policy review.

> Security Administrators shall maintain Risk Acceptance Memos for each waiver granted to these policies. Managers who want to ignore a part of these policies must sign that memo accepting responsibility for the security of those systems and networks.

Publishing and Notification Requirements of the Policies

After the policies have been written, they will not do your organization any good if they sit on the shelf collecting dust. Not only should it be a living document, but it also should be accessible to all users. A common way of doing this is to publish the policies on the organization's intranet. This way, not only are the policies available to all users, but your organization will save on printing costs—and updates can be made in one central location without having to ensure they are distributed.

Policies in this area should cover both the publishing of the policy documents and notification of when published. This policy also should cover who is responsible for these acts. Many organizations tend to leave these responsibilities up to the Human Resources Department. However, some smaller companies and those that have out-sourced their Human Resources Departments might have to designate another publisher. One version of this type of policy can say

> *The Human Resources Department shall be responsible for publishing these Information Security Policies and all updates on the organization's intranet to make it easily accessible by everyone.*

> *When these policies or updates are published, the Human Resources Department shall notify every user that the policies have been published and how they may be accessed.*

One company I worked with was concerned about what would happen if the electronic copy were inaccessible. After all, servers do crash, network equipment can fail, and the intranet might not be accessible by some remote users. They wanted a policy to require a printed version be available in all departments and anywhere that did not have access to the intranet. To do that, we came up with a policy that said

> *The Human Resources Department shall be responsible for providing each depart-ment and others without access to the intranet one printed copy of these policies at the same time as the publishing of the electronic version.*

Monitoring, Controls, and Remedies

The most controversial section of any information security policy outlines the type of monitoring, controls, and remedies for violations. The controversy arises from some of the monitoring and control policies that can be used in enforcing information security. Although legal, privacy advocates see some of these methods as a violation of an indi-vidual's privacy rights. In my work with many organizations, I suggest that they be careful and create a policy that *implements* rather than one that suggests mistrust.

A problem with this is that statistics show that most security violations come from within the organization, even though the mainstream press focuses on external events. Because of the publicity, many policies have sufficient provisions for enforcing the pol-icy against outsiders. You need to look past the outside threat and consider the internal threat. Even though you do not want the policy to read like you are creating a police state, it should provide the ability to monitor and enforce these provisions.

Monitoring

The first step in creating monitoring policy is to establish the organization's right to monitor. Although this policy may be geared toward the management's right to monitor, the policy may say that management can assign someone to do the monitoring. After all, few organizations' lead information technology executives will sit in front of a monitor actually monitoring network traffic. This policy can read

> *Management shall be allowed to monitor all systems activities and network traffic to enforce the provisions of these policies. Management shall be allowed to assign monitoring and other duties to appropriate administrators.*

Controlling

Control policies establish the organization's right to establish mechanisms to install appropriate controls. Although other policies do allow the organization to set up access controls, user and password requirements, these policies establish the right to implement their provisions. As unusual as this seems, a few attorneys have suggested that this may be necessary to avert potential problems if the organization is sued. Even if the courts in your organization's jurisdiction may not require this, it will not hurt to include these provisions. Such a policy can simply say

> *Management shall install controls consistent with the requirements of these policies.*

Along with control, the policy has to concern itself with who can administer and test these controls. Organizations do not want anyone to test their security measures without anyone's knowledge. With the availability of free tools via the Internet, the danger of this happening increases by users who are curious or those looking to intentionally break security.

The Case of Randal Schwartz

In a famous case, noted author and Perl expert Randal Schwartz was convicted of a computer crime in Oregon for, among other things, unauthorized testing of security measures on Intel's network and systems while working for Intel as a contractor. Schwartz claims to have done this with good intentions. Regardless of how you feel about this case, consider what you would think if you were responsible for the security of the network. You could never know if the probes were being made for honorable or dishonorable intentions, especially if the allegedly honorable person was doing this without permission. How would you know? How would you handle this situation? Consider this when writing your policy.

The wording of these policies is highly dependent on the laws governing your jurisdiction. For these policies to be effective and, if necessary, enforceable by law, the legal code or case law may have requirements you must follow for your policies to withstand legal scrutiny. I know this is not how technical people think, but you must change your mindset and ask legal counsel for assistance. The following statements can be used as a guide to establish the control policies:

> *Management and assigned administrators shall have the responsibility of testing access controls and the network for vulnerabilities. Users shall not test for vulnerabilities and access controls by manual or programmatic means.*

> *When vulnerabilities are known, users shall not exploit their effects by manual or programmatic means.*

> *Management and assigned administrators shall have access to the tools that can help manage and test information security. Users shall not have access to these tools on the organization's network. Users shall not load or download these tools from any location.*

Remedies

Along with every rule and every law, there are suggested guidelines for sentencing and penalties. For the information security policies, you also should have a statement regarding remedies. One reason is that if there happens to be a case where a security has been violated, there can be no questions whether your organization has the right to seek these remedies. Because the violation can happen from within the organization or by an external attacker, the policy should be written to cover both.

In the jurisdictions I have been working, establishing these policies starts with a general statement saying that the user is not allowed to do harm to the systems, network, or others. The statement can be worded in a way that could capture the essence of the enforcement provisions for all the policies. This statement can say

> *Any conduct which adversely affects the ability of others to use the company's systems and networks or which can harm or offend others shall not be permitted.*

Next, establish the policy of the organization to have remedies for users who violate the policy. I like to use two statements. One policy statement is directed at the users. I use this to address remedies to internal users, such as employees. The other statement is similar but targeted at external users or contractors who are using the network by special permission. This policy should address the nature of their usage, such as acknowledging contracts or agreements that give them access. One example that I used locally read

> *Management shall have the right to revoke any user's access privileges and terminate their association with the organization at any time for violations of this policy or conduct that disrupts the normal operation of the organization's network and computing systems.*

> *Management shall have the right to sever contracts and agreements with contractors and other outside users if they violate this policy or demonstrate conduct that disrupts the normal operation of the organization's network and computing systems.*

Finally, policies should cover illegal activities perpetrated by inside users and outside attackers. In my jurisdiction, I can write a single policy statement that covers the organization's response to all illegal activities. There are no shortcuts to this policy. It must say, in a manner consistent with local law, what will happen if there are legal violations.

A client who wanted the option to involve law enforcement and the legal system, rather than make it mandatory, used the following sample statement. Management felt that in some cases dismissal of an employee was enough of a remedy. Because this was covered in the previous policy statement, we wrote a policy that said

> *Management shall have the right to exercise their options under the appropriate criminal and civil laws to seek legal remedies from anyone who uses, abuses, or attacks the organization's network and information systems in a manner that would be in violation of the law and these policies.*

Administrator's Responsibility

The previous section of this chapter concentrated more on the management responsibility of enforcing the policies. Management might assign some of the monitoring and compliance issues to administrators, but those are left as implementation details. In the administrator's policies, you should outline the areas for which the administrator will be responsible.

Some of the policies are not just for the Systems, Network, and Security Administrators. Administrative policies also can outline administrative responsibilities that are the responsibility of data and process owners as well as those responsible for users. These policies cover the administrative compliance and enforcement issues of the policies that fall outside the realm of management control.

Depending on the depth and breadth of your policies, the number of issues that should have policies can seem overwhelming. Before writing these policies, figure out what should be under administrative policies. For example, here is a short list of suggested topics:

- Periodically reviewing and reauthorizing user access privileges for employees and contractors
- Requiring positive identification of all users, even if assigned to other managers or human resources
- Identifying who may create user identification for the systems and networks
- Maintaining a master database or directory of user identification and access privileges
- Handling the changing of privileges and duties
- Managing tools used to assist in complying with these policies
- Verifying compliance when systems are brought online or updated
- Establishing naming conventions for systems and other network components

One policy I would like to discuss is what happens when an employee or contractor is no longer associated with the organization. Regardless of whether the termination is from voluntary or involuntary means, administrators must have procedures in place to revoke access to the organization's resources. Keeping a user's identification active might leave the network open for attack.

Procedures for handling terminated users are beyond the scope of the policy documents. However, the policies can place the responsibility for dealing with the issues surrounding terminating users. Some of the issues that could be included are identifying who is responsible for ensuring that access is revoked in a timely manner, releasing of resources allocated to the user, examining the user's resources for security and other violations, and archiving user files and other data. A simplified policy statement that covers revocation and archiving can say

> *Users whose association with the organization has been terminated shall have their access privileges to the organization's resources immediately revoked. Administrators shall arrange for the programs and other data used by these users archived. Administrators shall create procedures for revoking access of these users.*

Logging Considerations

Regardless of how diligent your organization is when it comes to monitoring security, the majority of violations will be discovered after they occur. In most cases, administrators will see the evidence of violations without witnessing their occurrence. One method administrators use to review system activity is to examine the logs that systems and major software packages generate. The logs produced by these components can log everything users do on a system or network, or they can log errors or certain successful accesses, such as administrative users being granted access to systems.

Logging policies are difficult because you cannot write one statement that fits every environment. While it can be impractical to log every command executed on a computer system, it might be necessary for the maintenance of database services. Policies could say that logging will include relevant events, but how does anyone define "relevant" across all networks and systems? Then, for some systems in some organizations, logging might be optional. For example, a print server might have logging turned off because the printing services may keep that information elsewhere.

When considering logging policies, the policy should consider a statement that requires the inclusion of security-relevant events in the logs. This could ensure that the forensic information needed to understand how the security violations manifested themselves is available. Obviously this might not be all the information used in this role, but it is necessary. Other considerations include:

- Logs must support auditing in a manner consistent with the system that generates their entries.
- Logs must supply enough information to support accountability and traceability for all privilege system commands.

- Logs should include a record of user-initiated, security-relevant activities.
- For databases, logs might be required to be able to reconstruct production information.

Another area of logging policies should describe the handling of the logs. Because of their importance in the security monitoring process, policy guidelines for handling logs are crucial in ensuring that they are available for administrators. Some have argued that these policies are common sense and that administrators do not need these policies. I tend not to assume that everyone will understand what is inferred, so I suggest that they be included. A generic set of policy statements to support this can say

Administrators shall review the system and other logs on a regular basis.

Only authorized users shall review log files.

Administrators shall take appropriate precautions to prevent logs from being deactivated, modified, or deleted.

Administrators shall follow appropriate procedures when they discover violations of these policies or network security.

In regard to the last policy statement, although creating procedures to produce logs is easy, they are the most difficult to implement. The problem is not in collecting the information—that is relatively simple—but it is truly an art to methodically work through the logs and determine what has really transpired. This takes a lot of skill and time.

Finally, policies should consider what to do with the logs as time passes. Administrators recognize that logs must be rotated and even removed from the systems to ensure the system can capture the events being logged. This type of control should have a policy that mandates rotation and retention policies. These policies should consider the system space and resource requirements as well as requirements that may be placed on how long logs should be maintained.

Retention policies can vary from types of organizations based on their industries to the types of logs being retained. For example, financial organizations might have to retain up to 10 years of logs from their financial transactions so that they may be audited in the future. Additionally, policies might be required regarding the handling of the disposition of these logs. These policies may be similar to those considered for backup policies that were discussed in Chapter 2, "Determining Your Policy Needs."

Reporting of Security Problems

Enforcement of these policies should be everyone's responsibility, not just the administrator's. Earlier policies have provisions for users to assist in their enforcement, but none define the full impact of that reporting. Writing the policies for reporting is like all the other policies in this chapter—they are highly dependent on the environment and legal requirements for enforcing the policies.

Handling of Information Security Incident Reporting

Incident reports can come from a number of sources. Administrators can find security problems, and policies can be in place for users to report violations. Incidents can be reported outside the organization through other administrations reporting problems that seem to emanate from your site, law enforcement, or by audits, to name a few. Finally, there are public disclosures of problems that can come from the vendor or incident response groups.

The first of these policies establishes the reporting requirements of both administrators and users. When writing these policies, I like to include a statement requiring that the reporting follow procedures. This puts the onus on someone to devise the procedures. This can be written as follows:

> Administrators and users shall report all violations to these policies and associated procedures using the designated reporting procedures.

Then the policies need to consider what happens when the report comes from outside sources. Most organizations I have worked with want these reports taken seriously and want them investigated. Using that as a mandate, you can write a policy that says:

> Administrators shall take reports from all outside sources seriously and investigate their validity. Discoveries from these investigations shall be handled using the established policies.

This policy does not consider what to do if the outside report is from law enforcement. Most organizations seem to want special handling when the police knock on their doors with problems. One organization I worked with wanted the policy to make management directly responsible for everything regarding an investigation instigated by law enforcement. This policy can present problems if the management person in charge does not know enough about information security to lead the investigation. For these policies, the organization chose to make a statement, knowing it would have to write specific procedures later. A paraphrase of that statement read

> The response of violations from law enforcement shall be coordinated with management. Management shall be the lead internal investigator and shall take responsibility for interfacing and cooperating with law enforcement.

The final aspect of reporting policy is what to do with public disclosure reports from vendors and incident response organizations. There is a lot of controversy as to which incident response organizations to accept as the source of potential problems. Some say to listen to the vendors, who also are criticized for being slow to respond. Others look to a number of other organizations, such as the CERT Coordination Center (CERT/CC) for credible information. However, CERT/CC has been criticized for not reporting every incident. And this does not consider virus reports provided from the anti-virus vendors.

This makes public disclosure policies difficult to write. Policy writers have the tendency to want to include every incident response organization to ensure that all bases are covered. Rather than write an all-inclusive policy, the statement can provide the guidance that would go into procedures that can be changed as requirements change. To do this, the policy can say

> *Administrators shall monitor public disclosure organizations that report incidents, bugs, and other problems that could affect the security of the organization's network and systems. These public disclosure organizations shall include the vendors of the information systems in use by the organization, at least two general organizations, and the vendor of the organization's chosen anti-virus software.*

Required Actions

After incidents are reported, there is an evidence gathering and enforcement responsibility that must support the report. It is not enough to say that something happened. If the incident requires some sort of remedy that involves disciplinary actions or law enforcement, a policy must outline the requirements for handling this evidence.

Some of these policies require knowledge of handling evidence given that they will be required for law enforcement. There are some general policy statements that can be written. When writing these statements, consider policies that would handle the following:

- In general, a policy to capture information related to the security or policy violation. The policy can be written in a way as to leave the details up to implementation, thus avoiding the legal problems.

- Amplification of policies regarding the reporting and eradication of virus infestation.

- How to report and act upon required reporting of software malfunctions and other bugs.

- Isolating potential problems when incident reporting groups report problems.

Auditing and Data Capturing

Over the course of time, administrators will collect a lot of data. Whether the data comes from logs or from snapshots of systems and network traffic, this data can be used to audit the effectiveness of the policies. As part of the periodic audit for evaluating the policy, this data can be useful in learning about problems that are caused by or as a result of these policies.

I have found that having this data is useful for learning about the organization and how to craft or update its policies. As a side effect, they also can provide network usage information that can help the organization make changes that can then make the network more efficient. Therefore, auditing policies also should include the necessity to retain the information for consideration. The policy simply can say

> *Data regarding information security violations and incident handling shall be retained so that it may be used during the analysis of the information security policies.*

Considerations When Computer Crimes Are Committed

Computer crimes have become a focal point of security enforcement over the last few years. As organizations focus on security and have been taking their information assets more seriously, there has been a public outcry to prosecute those who commit crimes with computers. With this focus, the U.S. Congress, many states, and even international governments like the European Union have passed laws to help fight computer crime.

Still, dealing with computer crimes is not easy. Although some law enforcement agencies have been trying to educate themselves in dealing with this new frontier, only the FBI seems to be able to commit the resources necessary to solve some crimes. However, their resources are limited, and they put a lower limit on the amount of damage caused by the crime before they will investigate.

Not every organization will want to report computer crime. If this information is disclosed, the organization faces embarrassment and possible repercussions from a market that might turn the organization's victimization into mistrust. A major bank experienced significant shareholder fallout when it was disclosed that an attacker stole $10 million through the Internet. The only reason that bank made the disclosure was under court order. Otherwise, we never would have known.

Working with Law Enforcement

If your organization plans to work with law enforcement, you need to find out how you can work with them. First, not every law enforcement department is capable of handling a computer crime investigation. Most local police departments cannot handle the requirements to do this type of investigation. For those in the United States, your investigation will fall on the FBI.

There is no formula for working with any law enforcement organization. Before writing policies, you might want to contact your local law enforcement bureau or the FBI field office to learn what they require for your organization to report a crime. Use that information for writing your policy.

Consideration for Preservation of Evidence

Law enforcement still works under the principals of physically securing the area and working their way into a crime scene. Unfortunately, computer crimes cannot be cordoned off with the ubiquitous yellow tape. However, to prosecute computer crimes, the preservation of evidence to prove the case is essential—depending on the requirements of law enforcement and the government attorney who would prosecute the offenders.

To write policies in this area, all aspects of dealing with the law enforcement community should be reviewed to determine policy requirements. For large organizations whose facilities span multiple locations, you must consider problems with jurisdiction as well as the idiosyncrasies of the laws associated with each location. And the rules are completely different for the various local, state, and federal government agencies. Sometimes, the best thing to do is write a simple policy saying that the organization will work with law enforcement as appropriate. The details can be left to the associated procedures after you have a discussion with your local District Attorney's office.

Summary

To ensure the systems and networks are protected, compliance and enforcement policies define what could happen when policy is broken. Compliance and enforcement policies tend to fall outside the technical arena in which most security professionals work. These policies require knowledge of various corporate policies as well as compliance to various laws, including intellectual property, labor, and possibly criminal law.

1. Testing and effectiveness of the policies:

    - Compliance is a very subjective process. Policies in this section will cover the notification and report processes with your measurements.

    - Management should encourage security-awareness training so that everyone in the organization understands the policies and their impact.

    - Policies can include a statement on general measures that can be used to test the policy's effectiveness.

2. Publishing and notification requirements of the policies:

    - Publishing policies should cover both the publishing of the policy documents and notification of when published.

    - These policies also should cover who is responsible for these acts.

3. Monitoring, controls, and remedies:

    - The first step in creating monitoring policy is to establish the organization's right to monitor.

    - Control policies establish the organization's right to establish mechanisms to install appropriate controls. The policy should concern itself with who can administer and test these controls.

    - The policy should establish suggested guidelines for remedies. It leaves no question as to whether your organization has the right to seek remedies for violations.

    - Policies should cover illegal activities that occur by inside users as well as outside attackers.

4. Administrator's responsibility:

   - Administrative policies also can outline administrative responsibilities that are the responsibility of data and process owners as well as those responsible for users. These policies cover the administrative compliance and enforcement issues of the policies that fall outside the realm of management control.

   - Policies for handling the occasions when an employee or contractor is no longer associated with the organization consider identifying who is responsible for ensuring that access is revoked in a timely manner, releasing of resources allocated to the user, examining the user's resources for security and other violations, and archiving user files and other data.

5. Logging considerations:

   - One mechanism administrators use to review system activity is to examine the logs that systems and major software packages generate.

   - The logs produced by these components can log everything users do on a system or network, or they can log errors or certain successful accesses, such as administrative users being granted access to systems.

   - Logging policies are difficult because you cannot write one statement that fits every environment. It may be impractical to log every command executed on a computer system, but it may be necessary for the maintenance of database services. Policies could say that logging must include relevant events, but how does anyone define "relevant" across all networks and systems?

   - Another area of logging policies should describe the handling of the logs.

   - Log retention policies can vary from types of organizations based on their industries to the types of logs being retained.

6. Reporting of security problems:

   - Incident reports can come from a number of sources. Administrators can find security problems, and policies can be in place for users to report violations.

   - Policies establish the reporting requirements of both administrators and users.

   - Most organizations seem to want special handling when the police knock on their doors with problems.

   - Policies for handling public disclosure reports should include a diversity of information for both coverage and verification.

   - After incidents are reported, there is an evidence gathering and enforcement responsibility that must support the report. It is not enough to say that something happened. If the incident requires some sort of remedy that involves disciplinary actions or law enforcement, a policy must outline the requirements for handling this evidence.

7. Considerations when computer crimes are committed:

- Dealing with computer crimes is not easy. Although some law enforcement agencies have been trying to educate themselves in dealing with this new frontier, only the FBI seems to be able to commit the resources necessary to solve some crimes.

- Before writing these policies, you might want to contact your local law enforcement bureau or the FBI field office to learn what they require for when your organization needs to report a crime.

- To be able to prosecute computer crimes, the preservation of evidence to prove the case is essential—depending on the requirements of law enforcement and the government attorney who would prosecute the offenders. It might be necessary to consult with the local District Attorney or Attorney General to understand evidentiary requirements before writing policies.

13

The Policy Review Process

YOUR ORGANIZATION'S POLICIES ARE NOW IN EFFECT. Users are being trained, incidents are occurring, and everyone is aware of the information security requirements. But we know that the security policy is only as good as the ability to enforce its provisions. Even in the best of worlds, you will discover that these documents will have policies that hinder the business process and some that do not go far enough.

Security policy documents should be living documents. They should change and evolve as your organization grows and technology changes. To keep up, these policies must undergo periodic review; and to ensure that this is a perpetual process, the final policy you write is the one that will establish the review process. This is a process that will incorporate the information collected and learned as part of enforcement.

Periodic Reviews of Policy Documents

There is no rule as to how often policy documents are reviewed. When I work with organizations, I suggest that they be reviewed sometime between six months and one year. Six months seems like enough time to see if patterns exist that require policy adjustment (see the sidebar, "Recognizing Security Patterns"). However, some believe that a longer period is necessary. But if you let it go longer than a year, you could run the risk of having problems fester—thus causing a disrespect for the policies and leading to them being ignored.

Recognizing Security Patterns

While administrators monitor and enforce the policies, they may discover that waiver requests are made under similar circumstances or that audit logs show repetitive attempts at violations of policies. There are many ways to find patterns in the waivers, logs, and violation reports. Some commercial packages, such as intrusion detection systems, have statistical analysis add-on modules that will help. Other systems, like mainframes, provide these analysis tools as part of the operating system's utilities.

However, automated tools might not be sufficient. Administrators will have to use inspection and intuition to find patterns that are dependent on understanding your network's usage patterns. For example, under UNIX, you might see several attempts to log in as *root*, the "superuser" account. Although the several attempts were made by different users, they appear to be from the same terminal or remotely from the same system on the network. This pattern could indicate an attempt to break in to the system from one that was compromised. However, if the remote system is primarily used by your organization's developers, they could be attempting to diagnose and fix a problem.

The result of this analysis might be a policy that allows developers to gain *root* access or make *root* access available when necessary. However, the only way to determine this is to associate the violation with how the systems or network is used.

Organizations that are writing their first policy worry about whether their policies will really provide the backbone to a solid information security program. For those organizations, I suggest that the policy be reviewed every six months for the first few years. The side effect of this process is that you do not have to include this type of time limit in your review policy. The policy can be changed at a subsequent review session when the reviewers believe that the policy is stable enough to wait a longer time between reviews. To establish the review process, the policy statement can simply say:

These information security policies shall undergo a review every six months.

As we all know, networks and computers can be unpredictable in the hands of humans. Even the best policy writers will omit something because it is impossible to predict everything that could happen. The enforcement and waiver provisions should allow for a certain amount of latitude to protect the network, but inevitably, something can, and will, be outside the scope of the policies. For example, a small organization that is now selling the newest hot product has established a partnership with another organization. As part of the partnership agreement, both organizations will share information about each other so that both can extend each other's product. The agreement requires that both organizations share their information via a Virtual Private Network (VPN) connection. However, your organization did not anticipate this type of arrangement and does not have a policy for working with VPNs.

When changes occur quickly, some organizations opt for issuing a policy waiver or variance (see Chapter 3, "Information Security Responsibilities"). A waiver is an agreement signed by the data or process owner saying that the basis for the security process will be based on an a specific update to the existing policy as outlined in the new document. In this example, that waiver could specify that the VPN connection be treated similarly to an Internet connection with some additional restriction. Another way to do this is to have a policy with a provision to establish an ad hoc review process when it is necessary to add new or update certain policies in an emergency situation. This policy can say

> *Management shall form an ad hoc review committee to create, update, or review policies when significant changes are necessary prior to the regular review.*

What the Policy Reviews Should Include

The first three chapters of this book set the groundwork for creating these policies. In those chapters, I also suggest that this type of support should go into the review process. One of the reasons I said this is to leverage much of the information that was collected during the authoring process. Over the course of time, operations and the procedures created to support these policies will refine that research and create additional information that should provide additional input to the review process.

One of the most important elements to include in the review is the information gained from a risk assessment or audit. As I discussed in Chapter 1, "What Information Security Policies Are," the risk assessment and audit can be a good way to obtain a broad assessment of the impact of security and the policies on your organization's network. I also strongly suggested that an outsider, someone who does not have a stake in its result, perform the risk assessment. This is the best way to ensure an impartial look into the effectiveness of the entire security plan.

Other useful information that should be included in the process is the business intelligence and the business process information brought to the review by management. Management holds a key to the direction of the organization and can use this knowledge to ensure that the policies support the organization as it grows. For example, if management knew about the negotiations that would create the partnership described earlier in this chapter, they could provide guidance for creating a VPN policy that would be in place in time to implement the agreement.

Although some information might seem insignificant, it should be considered during the review process to determine its relevance. The most significant data can come from the Network and Systems Administrators. The administrators are in daily contact with the users. They hear about the struggles incurred daily. The policy review team can use this information to understand how the policy impacts their usage of the network and their ability to get their work done. Managers can bring the input of their users and the impression from customers if there have been problems that need to be addressed. Everyone should come together with this information along with suggestions as to how to improve the policies to prevent future problems.

Everyone also should remember what worked. Policies can aid in opening opportunities brought about by new configurations, connections, and the trust built by being able to demonstrate the ability to secure network transactions. These inputs can be used to prevent an overreaction to problems.

The Review Committee

Ideally, the review committee would consist of representatives from all stakeholders affected by the policies. These are the same stakeholders that were involved in writing the policies. Aside from the executives, managers, and the various information technology administrators, the committee also should include a representative of the organization's Human Resources Department and an attorney. If the review is examining policies that requires certain legal knowledge, such as encryption policies, then an attorney versed in those laws should either be present or consulted regarding the changes.

In reality, some organizations might have problems convening a committee. Smaller organizations whose resources are stretched thin might not be in a position to commit resources even if they realize that it is necessary. Organizations that can commit the resources should do so. Even if you cannot convene a meeting of every stakeholder, a fair representation can be just as good.

Organizations that cannot commit resources for a review committee can use more creative ways to review the policy. A year after helping a small organization (with less than 50 users) write its policies, they asked me to help coordinate their review process. Rather than physically meeting, I coordinated discussions via email. After the result of a security audit was forwarded to all stakeholders, they were asked to email suggestions for policy changes. I coordinated the suggestions and led discussions using a moderated mailing list.

When the committee reached consensus on the topic, I wrote the policy change and sent it via the mailing list to the committee for a vote. I tallied the result and started the next discussion. After six weeks of discussions and votes, the committee made three changes to their policies and everyone went away pleased with their work and the process.

With the policies completed and a review process in place, the job of securing the organization's network has only begun. Security administrators must now start to create or update procedures and begin to enact these measures with the ability to monitor and enforce these policies. Information security should be a proactive process, not a reactive one.

Summary

Security policy documents should be living documents, changing and evolving as the organization and technology changes. Policies must undergo periodic review to ensure they are kept up to date. The final policy you write is the one that will establish the review process that will incorporate the information collected as part of enforcement.

1. Periodic reviews of policy documents:

   - There is no rule as to how often the policy documents are reviewed. However, it is suggested that they be reviewed sometime between six months and one year.

   - A provision of the review process should include the ability to create an ad hoc review committee when there is an immediate requirement for a significant change to the policies.

2. What the policy reviews should include:

   - The information collected during the authoring process will continue to be valuable.

   - Data collected while enforcing the policies and procedures that were created as a result of these policies.

   - The information collected from a risk assessment or audit.

   - Management can bring the business process and business intelligence as input.

   - Even hearsay information as to how everyone feels about the policies and resulting procedures can yield important information.

3. The review committee:

   - Ideally, the review committee will consist of representatives from all stakeholders affected by the policies. These are the same stakeholders that were involved in writing the policies.

   - Smaller organizations may not be able to commit the resources necessary to do a review. These organizations can try creative methods rather than organizing meetings.

IV

Appendixes

Glossary

THESE DEFINITIONS WILL GIVE YOU A BASIC understanding of the terms used throughout this book. As with many technical definitions, more information may be required to fully understand the concepts. A good place to find detailed definitions to these and other technical terms is at http://www.whatis.com.

Acceptable Use Policy (AUP) A policy that the user agrees to follow before being allowed to access a network.

access control list (ACL) A table used by systems and systems software to define access rights.

ActiveX The object-oriented language from Microsoft used to create mobile code.

air gap A term used to describe the absolute separation of two or more networks.

anti-virus A class of software that attempts to prevent computer viruses from infecting a system.

applet A small program that is delivered from a server and run on the client's computer.

asymmetric encryption See "public key cryptography."

attack scenario Part of survivable network analysis. Attack scenarios define how a system could be attacked.

AUP See "Acceptable Use Policy."

authentication The process of determining whether someone or something is who or what it is declared to be.

backdoor In software design, the mechanism programmed to allow the programmer special access to the software.

biometrics The technologies for measuring and analyzing human body characteristics to authenticate someone.

Bootstrap Protocol (BOOTP) A protocol that lets a network machine automatically receive a network address when the operating system boots or is initialized. BOOTP is the basis for the Dynamic Host Configuration Protocol (DHCP).

bounds checking A software development method that checks the boundaries of internal memory operations to prevent problems, such as buffer overflows.

BSA See "Business Software Alliance."

buffer overflow A common software problem that could be prevented with bounds checking, where an internal memory operation writes data in areas outside its boundaries.

Bureau of Export Affairs (BXA) The bureau of the U.S. Federal Trade Commission that implements the administration's policy on encryption export.

Business Software Alliance (BSA) An international industry organization whose main purpose is to fight software piracy.

BXA See "Bureau of Export Affairs."

CGI See "Common Gateway Interface."

Commercial Off-The-Shelf (COTS) Describes products that can be readily purchased from commercial entities.

Common Gateway Interface (CGI) A standard used to pass data from a client (for example, a browser) to a web server to be processed by a particular program on the server.

contingency planning The act of creating procedures to ensure that the network, systems, and data are not lost in the event of an outage or disaster. The result of contingency planning is the Disaster Recovery Plan.

copyright The exclusive legal right to reproduce, publish, and sell a piece of intellectual property. Copyrights do not have to be registered, but it helps when trying to protect them in the courts.

COTS See "Commercial Off-The-Shelf."

cryptographic hash A function that uses cryptographic functions to transform data into a unique, fixed-length value that cannot be converted back into the original data.

data ownership The concept of who owns the data for the purposes of assigning security responsibilities.

DDoS See "Distributed Denial of Service."

decryption The process of converting encrypted data back into its original form.

demilitarized zone (DMZ) A network segment that is placed between the organization's network and a public network, usually the Internet. Public network services, such as DNS and web servers, are usually installed on the DMZ.

denial of service (DoS) An attack on a system or network that prevents users from accessing its resources.

DHCP See "Dynamic Host Configuration Protocol."

digital certificate A small bit of data issued by a certification authority that contains information about who the certificate was issued to, as well as the certifying authority that issued it. Digital certificates contain the public key used in public key cryptography.

digital signature Cryptographic hashes created by using the private key in the digital certificate. Digital signatures can be verified using the signer's public key, which may be kept by the certification authority.

Distributed Denial of Service (DDoS) When more than one system is used to attack the resources of a single server to create a denial-of-service attack.

Disaster Recovery Plan (DRP) The procedures created from contingency planning to ensure that networks, systems, and databases are not lost in the event of an outage or disaster. Some DRPs include procedures for continuous operations in the event of an outage.

DMZ See "demilitarized zone."

Domain Name Service (DNS) The server that translates the readable domain name to an IP address.

DoS See "Denial of Service."

DRP See "Disaster Recovery Plan."

duress password A special password assigned to administrative accounts that will signal the user logged in under duress. The purpose is to have the system contact or notify an authority to handle the problem.

Dynamic Host Configuration Protocol (DHCP) A protocol that allows Network Administrators to centrally manage and automate the assignment of Internet Protocol (IP) addresses on an organization's network.

Electronic Data Interchange (EDI) A standard format for trading partners to exchange business data. An EDI message contains strings of data elements, each representing a singular item. The entire string is called a data segment. One or more data segments can be grouped together to form a transaction set. These transaction sets usually contain elements that would appear in a typical business document or form.

encryption The conversion of data into a form that cannot be easily understood by unauthorized people.

exploit An attack on a computer system that takes advantage of a particular vulnerability.

extranet A private network that uses the Internet protocol and the public Internet to securely extend the organization's intranet, making it accessible to partners, customers, vendors, and so on.

Federal Information Processing Standards (FIPS) Standards used by U.S. federal agencies to define their information-processing environment. FIPS Publications are the documentation of the standards maintained by National Institute of Standards and Technology (NIST).

FIPS Pub 140-2 *Security Requirements* for *Cryptographic Modules*, the standard for using encryption with U.S. federal agencies.

firewall A device or program that protects a network. Firewalls are placed at network gateways to prevent unwanted or malicious traffic from entering the organization's network and block unauthorized traffic from leaving the internal network.

Frame Relay A telecommunication service designed to connect local area networks (LANs). These are called endpoints on the Frame Relay network. Frame Relay works by packaging data in variable-sized packets (frames) and transmitting them to the associated end-point.

All error correction is left to the endpoints, which speeds up overall data transmission.

gateway A point on a network that acts as an entrance to another network.

hacker A term used by programmers to mean a good programmer. When used by the mainstream media, it means anyone who breaks into systems and networks without authorization or who uses computers to commit fraud.

hub A device where network traffic comes together before being distributed out to connected systems or other networks.

ICMP See "Internet Control Message Protocol."

IETF See "Internet Engineering Task Force."

incident response The policies and procedures for responding to a security problem or breach.

industrial espionage The stealing of trade secrets from one company by another or by a foreign government.

information assets The organization's data that creates value of the organization. In many organizations, information assets define the goals and mission.

Information Ownership The concept of assigning the responsibility to someone who will be responsible for the management and integrity of the data.

information security policies The statements that define the information security program.

intellectual property In the concept of information security, the data created by the organization that is being protected by the policies.

Internet Control Message Protocol (ICMP) An error-reporting and message-control protocol between Internet

hosts. ICMP uses IP datagrams transparent to the user and the user's application.

Internet Engineering Task Force (IETF) The volunteer organization that maintains the standards used on the Internet.

Internet Network Information Center (InterNIC) A cooperative between the U.S. government and Network Solutions, Inc. It was the organization responsible for registering and maintaining the top-level domain names. Today, a nonprofit global organization, the Internet Corporation for Assigned Names and Numbers (ICANN), was formed to monitor the registrar accreditation process.

interoperability The ability of software or systems to work with each other without special effort.

intranet A private network that is contained within an enterprise. The intranet can be a single network or several linked networks accessible only to the enterprise.

intruder Another name the mainstream media gives to a hacker.

intrusion detection A system that monitors system or network traffic to detect security violations.

Internetwork Packet Exchanged (IPX) A networking protocol from Novell that interconnects networks that use Novell's Netware software.

ISO 9001 A standard describing quality control standards of all business processes and procedures.

Java The object-oriented language used to create mobile code from Sun Microsystems.

Kerberos Developed as part of the Athena Project at the Massachusetts Institute of Technology (MIT). A secure method for authorizing requests on a computer network. Kerberos enables a user to request a "ticket" from an authorization process to be used to request a service from a server. Kerberos-aware services check the requesting ticket to determine access rights.

Man In The Middle Attack An attack where the message is intercepted and copied or modified before being transmitted to the intended recipient. Its purpose is to intercept authentication information or to falsify transmitted information such as financial transactions.

mobile code The term given to software that can be downloaded from a server and run on any system. ActiveX and Java are commonly used to create mobile code.

NAT See "Network Address Translation."

National Infrastructure Protection Center (NIPC) An investigation unit of the FBI whose jurisdiction is the nation's critical infrastructure, including the Internet.

National Institute of Standards and Technology (NIST) A bureau of the U.S. Department of Commerce. The Computer Security Resource Center maintains the information security standards for the federal government.

Netware A network operating system created by Novell, Inc. that supports IPX and IP networking protocols.

Network Address Translation (NAT) The translation of an IP address used within one network to a different IP address known within another network.

Network File System (NFS) A protocol that lets a computer use a disk on a remote computer as though it was mounted on the user's own computer.

NFS See "Network File System."

NIPC See "National Infrastructure Protection Center."

NIST See "National Institute of Standards and Technology."

open source Refers to any program whose source code is made available for public use or modification. Most open source software is developed as a public collaboration.

outsourcing An arrangement in which one company provides services that are normally provided internally for another organization.

packet The smallest transmission unit on a network.

password A unique series of characters that users enter to identify themselves to the system as part of the authentication process.

penetration testing The process of checking the security of a network's perimeter.

PKI See "public key infrastructure."

Point-to-Point Protocol (PPP) A protocol used for communications between two computers using a serial interface, usually over telephone lines.

PPP See "Point-to-Point Protocol."

privacy policy A statement that specifies how an organization will handle the private information it collects.

proxy server A service that acts as an intermediary between a user or service from the internal network and the Internet so that security can be ensured.

public key cryptography Based on a mathematical function that uses one key to encrypt a message and another to decrypt. One key is meant to be made public, the other one is kept private.

public key infrastructure (PKI) Enables users of insecure public networks to securely exchange data. PKI uses public and private key pairs generated using public key cryptography that is obtained from a trusted authority.

Request For Comments (RFC) A document from the IETF that defines or updates standards. Some RFC documents are written to provide information only.

risk assessment The review process to assess the security and vulnerability of a network.

router Software or device that examines the address within a packet and decides the path that a packet should take as it is forwarded toward its destination. Routers use tables that describe the state of network connections to decide how packets should be forwarded.

sendmail The popular open source program used to manage the transmission of Internet email.

servlet A small program that is run on a server.

shareware Software that is freely distributed with the understanding that if the user continues to use it after a certain amount of time, usually 30 days, the user will pay the author for its continued use.

Simple Mail Transfer Protocol (SMTP) The Level 5 protocol that is used to transmit email from one system to another.

spam Unsolicited, bulk email.

spoofing Part of a network attack where the attacker alters the IP address of the packet to one that the system being attacked trusts or will forward responses to.

stateful packet inspection A type of firewall filtering that maintains the state of incoming packets to prevent attacks

that rely on fragmentation of packets. Stateful packet inspection also can match replies to outbound requests to provide additional controls.

subnetwork A part of an organization's network. Usually, subnetworks are created to isolate network traffic from the rest of the network.

survivability The ability of a network computing system to provide essential services in the presence of attacks and failures and recover full services in a timely manner.

symmetric encryption A type of encryption where the same key is used to encrypt and decrypt data.

TCP See "Transmission Control Protocol."

telecommuting Working outside the traditional office using networking to connect the user to the organization's system.

transient connection A connection that is not permanent. Modem and wireless connections to a network are considered transient connections.

Transmission Control Protocol (TCP) A connection-oriented communications protocol that transmits messages between systems. TCP keeps up with the state of packet transmissions to ensure that all data arrives at the remote system and the remote system puts them together in order.

Trojan Horse A program in which malicious code is contained inside a program or data that appears harmless but can gain control and damage the computer.

tunneling A protocol that defines a specific virtual path that messages will travel over IP networks.

UDP See "User Datagram Protocol."

Usenet News A collection of messages organized into newsgroups that are transmitted over the Internet. Usenet News works using a store and forward system that distributes the postings to other servers. There is not a central Usenet server.

User Datagram Protocol (UDP) A connectionless communications protocol that transmits single units of data, called *datagrams,* between systems. UDP does not guarantee that datagrams will be received in the order sent, nor does it guarantee that the remote server will receive the datagrams.

Virtual Private Network (VPN) A private data network that uses the public telecommunication infrastructure, maintaining security through the use of a tunneling protocol and encryption.

virus Self-replicating malicious code that integrates itself into executable hosts such as boot sectors, programs, and macros. Viruses replicate when they are executed.

VPN See "Virtual Private Network"

vulnerability A weakness in the system that can be exploited by attackers. These weaknesses are usually caused by design flaws, bugs, or configuration errors in systems and supporting software.

Wassenaar Arrangement (WA) International armaments agreement that also has provisions for the import and export of encryption products.

Windows Internet Naming Service (WINS) A component of Microsoft Windows network services that maintains the translation of system names between Windows networking and IP addresses.

World Wide Web (WWW) "The World Wide Web is the universe of network-accessible information, an embodiment of human knowledge" (definition by web inventor, Tim Berners-Lee).

worm Self-replicating malicious code that replicates itself through networks. Worms may become apparent through harmful payloads or when the replication process gets out of control.

Resources

THESE RESOURCES COMPOSE A COLLECTION OF links that point to web sites, documents, and other information that you might find helpful in developing information security policies and managing your organization's information security program. Security information can come from a variety of places. These links point to many different types of sources that include many commercial, nonprofit, government, and "underground" resources. Use them to understand their unique perspectives on information security.

Incident Response Teams

The groups listed here provide information about security problems as they become known. In addition to reporting incidents, these groups work with various vendors and user organizations to keep them aware when problems occur. When fixes are available, each individual team reports them. They have their own level of services, which may include archiving of security software (source) and past incident reports.

- CERT Coordination Center (CERT/CC) (Carnegie Mellon University's Software Engineering Institute)—**http://www.cert.org**
- National Infrastructure Protection Center (sponsored by the Federal Bureau of Investigation)—**http://www.nipc.gov**

- Computer Incident Advisory Capability (sponsored by the U.S. Department of Energy)—**http://www.ciac.org/ciac**
- Federal Computer Incident Response Capability (FedCIRC) (sponsored by the U.S. General Services Administration)—**http://www.fedcirc.gov**
- Australian Computer Emergency Response Team (AusCERT)— **http://www.auscert.org.au**
- The German Research Network Computer Emergency Response Team (DFN-CERT) (This site is also available in English.)—**http://www.cert.dfn.de**

Other Incident Response Information

Other places to look for incidents are the services that monitor and disclose bugs in system software. Because many security problems are the result of exploiting bugs, it might be worth monitoring these sites and participating in their mailing lists.

- Bugtraq—A mailing list tracking bugs from all sources.—**http://www.security-focus.com**
- NT Bugtraq—Similar to Bugtraq except specific to the Windows NT operating system.—**http://www.ntbugtraq.com**
- Common Vulnerabilities and Exposures (CVE)—CVE aspires to describe and name all publicly known facts about computer systems that could allow somebody to violate a reasonable security policy for that system.— **http://cve.mitre.org**

Virus Protection

The following are web site links for most of the major virus-protection software vendors. If you are a user of the virus-protection program of that vendor, it is highly advisable to bookmark their page and take advantage of their free update services. This will allow you to stay on top of the latest attacks and protect your network. Virus protection is not a trivial task! Keeping up-to-date on the latest information and having an active virus-protection plan is the only way to keep your systems safe. Also your security plan should include a program that will make everyone aware of the necessity for virus protection and how to be proactive.

- Virus Bulletin (online publication, not vendor affiliated)—**http://www.virus-btn.com**
- Computer Associates Virus Information Center (InoculateIT)— **http://www.cai.com/virusinfo/**
- DataFellows F-Secure Virus Info Center—**http://www.datafellows.com/vir-info/**
- FRISK Software International (F-PROT and F-Stop)—**http://www.complex.is**

- McAfee Anti-Virus Emergency Response Team—**http://www.avertlabs.com**
- Norman Virus Control—**http://www.norman.no**
- ProLand Software Protector Plus—**http://www.pspl.com**
- Sophos Virus Information Center—**http://www.sophos.com/virusinfo**
- Symantec (Norton) AntiVirus Research Center—**http://www.symantec.com/ avcenter/index.html**
- TrendMicro Security Info - Virus Encyclopedia—**http://www.antivirus.com/ vinfo/index.htm**

Vendor-Specific Security Information

The following are web site links for each major operating and network systems vendor or user group for security issues concerning these systems. These are good sites to find vendor-specific fixes for various security problems. Note that web site addresses prefaced with an asterisk (*) are links directly to corporate home or support pages because that vendor does not provide a specific area for security or provides it on a subscription basis only.

- Caldera OpenLinux—**http://www.calderasystems.com/support/security**
- Cisco —***http://www.cisco.com/public/Support_root.shtml**
- Compaq—***http://www.compaq.com/support/default.html**
- Debian GNU/Linux—**http://www.debian.org/security/**
- FreeBSD—**http://www.freebsd.org/security/**
- Hewlett Packard—(US/Canada) ***http://us-support.external.hp.com/ index.html/ (Europe) *http://europe-support.external.hp.com/index.html/**
- IBM (all products and general info)—**http://www.ibm.com/security/**
- Microsoft—**http://www.microsoft.com/security/**
- Netscape —**http://home.netscape.com/security/index.html**
- NetBSD—**http://www.netbsd.org/Security/index.html**
- Novell—**http://www.novell.com/corp/security/**
- OpenBSD—**http://www.openbsd.com/security.html**
- Red Hat Linux—***http://www.redhat.com/support/**
- Santa Cruz Operation—**http://www.sco.com/security/**
- Silicon Graphics, Inc.—**http://www.sgi.com/support/security/index.html**
- Slackware Linux—***http://www.slackware.com**
- Sun Microsystems—**http://sunsolve.Sun.COM/pub-cgi/show.pl? target=security/sec**
- Java Security—**http://java.sun.com/security**

- S.u.S.E., Inc. (Linux)—**http://www.suse.de/de/support/security/index.html**
- Wind River Systems (including BSDI)—***http://www.windriver.com**

Security Information Resources

Following is a list of groups that provide significant information security resources. These resources consist of commercial, educational, and government-supported programs. The information is free and, for the most part, kept very current.

- @Stake Research Laboratories (the former L0pht Heavy Industries)— **http://www.atstake.com/research**
- About.com Network/Internet Security Forum—**http://netsecurity.about.com**
- CERIAS (Purdue University) for a good list of resources, visit the CERIAS HotList—**http://www.cerias.purdue.edu**
- CERT Coordination Center (Carnegie Mellon University)— **http://www.cert.org**
- Computer Crime and Intellectual Property Section (CCIPS) of the Criminal Division of the U.S. Department of Justice—**http://www.cybercrime.gov**
- Computer Security and Intelligence—**http://www.c4i.org**
- Computer Security Institute—**http://www.gocsi.com**
- Computer Security Resource Center (sponsored by NIST)— **http://csrc.nist.gov**
- Packet Storm—**http://www.packetstormsecurity.org**
- SANS Institute—**http://www.sans.org**
- Security Industry Association—**http://www.securitygateway.com**

Security Publications

These are printed magazines whose content is geared toward the information security professional. See their sites for subscription information.

- *Information Security*—**http://www.infosecuritymag.com**
- *SC: Information Security Magazine*—**http://www.scmagazine.com**

Industry Consortia and Associations

There have been many attempts to bring people and organizations together in order to promote information security among the masses. This is a list of some of those organizations that have been particularly active around the time this section was last edited.

- Chief Information Officers (CIO) Council—`http://www.cio.gov`
- CIO Institute—`http://www.cio.org`
- Forum of Incident Response Teams—`http://www.first.org`
- Information Security Forum—`http://www.securityforum.org`
- Internet Security Alliance—`http://www.isalliance.org`

Hacker and "Underground" Organizations

Not every hacker is a bad person. Not every "underground" organization is looking to take over the cyber world. However, I have found that the information on many of these sites is posted quicker than on so-called legitimate sites, and many times they describe the exploit better. Security professionals can learn a lot by reading the information these groups provide. I am *not* passing judgment on what these groups do with the information or how they obtain it. The sites here are a sample of those I read on a regular basis.

- *2600: The Hacker Quarterly*—`http://www.2600.com`
- ATTRITION—`http://www.attrition.org`
- Cult of the Dead Cow—`http://www.cultdeadcow.com`
- DefCon (Hacker's Conference)—`http://www.defcon.org`
- Digital Information Society—`http://www.phreak.org`
- Hacker's Home Page—`http://www.hackershomepage.com`
- Security Bugware—`http://oliver.efri.hr/~crv/security/bugs/list.html`
- UNIX/net/hack page—`http://www.unix.geek.org.uk/~arny/`

Health Insurance Portability and Accountability Act

The Health Insurance Portability and Accountability Act of 1996 (HIPAA) authorized the Secretary of Health and Human Services (HHS) to develop security and privacy standards to protect electronic healthcare information. The security and privacy standard were to cover processing, storing, and transmission of this data to prevent inadvertent or unauthorized use or disclosure of an individual's health information. The security and transaction standards were released in August 2000 and the privacy standards in April 2001. The healthcare industry has two years to bring their systems into compliance with HIPAA's regulations. Some HIPAA resources are as follows:

- The Health Insurance Portability and Accountability Act of 1996 (HIPAA) Page from the U.S. Department of Health and Human Services Health Care Financing Administration—`http://www.hcfa.gov/hipaa/hipaahm.htm`

- Phoenix Health Systems, a consulting firm specializing in healthcare information systems, sponsors this web site with comprehensive resources on HIPAA and HIPAA compliance.—**http://www.hipaadvisory.com**

- *HIPAA Security Policy Development: A Collaborative Approach*, by Miles M. Sato from the SANS Institute Reading Room, April 30, 2001— **http://www.sans.org/infosecFAQ/policy/HIPAA_policy.htm**

Survivability

"Survivability is the ability of a network computing system to provide essential services in the presence of attacks and failures, and recover full services in a timely manner."[1] The research into survivable systems is interesting because it attempts to move security past the accepted paradigm of building walls and creating passages through those barriers by concentrating on the business functions the system is supposed to support. The following links provide more information:

- Although there are others working on survivability research, the primary work is being initiated by the Software Engineering Institute at Carnegie Mellon University. You can read about their research and details of their survivability program at **http://www.cert.org/nav/index_purple.html**.

- The University of Virginia Department of Computer Science also has performed a lot of research into survivability through its Center for Survivable Information Systems. Their web site (**http://www.cs.virginia.edu/~survive/**) gives the reader another insight into how survivability fits into critical infrastructure protection.

- *Security By Itself May Not Be Enough—An Overview of the Discipline of System Survivability*, by John Price (May 10, 2001) clearly explains survivability and its role in information security clearly and in a manner that could be understood by a less-than-technical manager. The article is published in the SANS Information Security Reading Room and can be found at **http://www.sans.org/ infosecFAQ/securitybasics/not_enough.htm**.

Cryptography Policies and Regulations

Encryption is the only area of computing that is regulated through laws, policies, and treaties. Historically, all cryptography tools have been governed under the same rules as armaments. Under these rules, there is no difference between an anti-ballistic missile and the encryption that goes into protecting e-commerce transactions. In the United

---

1. R. J. Ellison, D. A. Fisher, R. C. Linger, H. F. Lipson, T. Longstaff, N. R. Mead. "Survivable Network Systems: An Emerging Discipline." *Technical Report CMU/SEI-97-TR-013, ESC-TR-97-013*. November 1997. Available from Internet: **http://www.cert.org/research/97tr013.pdf**

States, there are few rules regarding the import of encryption products, and U.S. users can use cryptography as they see fit. The problem comes when organizations require encryption to secure transmission with overseas offices. Even with the relaxing of regulations, exporting cryptography can still present a problem.

- In the United States, export controls on commercial encryption products are administered by the U.S. Department of Commerce, Bureau of Export Administration, Office of Strategic Trade and Foreign Policy Controls, and Information Technology Controls Division. Rules governing exports of encryption are found in the Export Administration Regulations (EAR), 15 C.F.R. Parts 730-774. More information can be found at **http://www.bxa.doc.gov/ Encryption/Default.htm**

- The Wassenaar Arrangement is an agreement among 33 countries to control exports for general arms and dual-use goods and technologies. One group of those technologies includes cryptography products. The web site for this agreement provides the basic rules and regulations of agreeing nations and contact information. You can find more information at **http://www.wassenaar.org**

Other good sources of information can be found at

- US Department of Justice FAQ on Encryption Policy—**http://www.cyber-crime.gov/cryptfaq.htm**

- *Crypto Law Survey* by Bert-Jaap Koops—**http://cwis.kub.nl/~frw/people/ koops/lawsurvy.htm**

- Security and cryptography expert Matt Blaze of AT&T Laboratories "Cryptography Resources on the Web"—**http://www.crypto.com**

- Counterpane Labs run by security and cryptography expert Bruce Schneier— **http://www.counterpane.com/labs.html**

Security Policy References

The following are references to various online resources that can be used to further assist in the writing of information security policies:

- Internet Engineering Task Force relevant Request for Comments (RFC) are available from the RFC Editor at **http://www.rfceditor.org**

  - RFC 2196—*Site Security Handbook*; B. Fraser, Editor, SEI/CMU; September 1997. **ftp://ftp.isi.edu/in-notes/rfc2196.txt**

  - RFC 2504—*Users' Security Handbook*; E. Guttman Sun Microsystems, L. Leong COLT Internet, G. Malkin Bay Networks; February 1999. **ftp://ftp.isi.edu/in-notes/rfc2504.txt**

  - RFC 2828—*Internet Security Glossary*; R. Shirey GTE/BBN Technologies; May 2000. **ftp://ftp.isi.edu/in-notes/rfc2828.txt**

- RFC 3013—*Recommended Internet Service Provider Security Services and Procedures*; T. Killalea neart.org; November 2000. `ftp://ftp.isi.edu/in-notes/rfc3013.txt`

- The SANS Institute Reading Room has several individual articles that focus on many areas of Information Security Policy development. The articles range from helping the reader define policy to working through implementation and validation details. These documents can be found at `http://www.sans.org/infosecFAQ/policy/policy_list.htm`

- *AusCERT Site Security Policy Development*, Rob McMillan, `ftp://ftp.auscert.org.au/pub/auscert/papers/Site.Security.Policy.Development.txt`

- A good example of a policy written for a university can be found at the University of California at Davis. Read their policy at `http://security.ucdavis.edu/policies`

- National Institute of Standards and Technology (NIST) maintains the security standards used by civilian agencies. The Guide for Developing Security Plans for Information Technology Systems, Special Publication 800-18 (SP 800-18), provides guidance to government agencies for developing security plans. SP 800-18 helps agencies comply with the regulations set forth by the Office of Management and Budget (OMB) Circular A-130 (Management of Federal Information Resources) Appendix III (Security of Federal Automated Information Resources). Those working with the US government on information security should read these documents to understand the agency's regulatory requirements. A copy of these documents can be found at

  - NIST SP 800-18—`http://csrc.nist.gov/publications/nistpubs/800-18/Planguide.PDF`

  - OMB Circular A-130 Appendix III—`http://www.whitehouse.gov/omb/circulars/a130/a130appendix_iii.html`

- Although the National Aeronautics and Space Administration (NASA) is not a civilian agency, they provide a good example of a security plan for one of their projects. You can read the NASA Integrated Services Network (NISN) Project Security Plan at `http://www.nisn.nasa.gov/Doc_Repos/secplan.html`

- Security policies and baseline standards are useless unless they are widely implemented. How you achieve this and how you manage your compliance will determine the success of your policies. The site from Security Risk Associates (of the UK) has a number of articles that discusses these issues. You can find them at `http://www.security.kirion.net/securitypolicy`

C

Sample Policies

THROUGHOUT THIS BOOK, I PROVIDE SAMPLE policy statements to illustrate what you can put into the policies you are writing. Individually, they are useful examples, but I know that people like full examples. This appendix has three examples of different policies that have been adopted from documents I worked on for various organizations.

If you remember, the sample statements in this book were written in a style that is similar to what you would see in a statement of work for a U.S. federal government contract. Some organizations do not like this style. Two of the policies do not follow this convention. I chose these samples to demonstrate how policies can be written using any language style.

The first sample, "Sample Acceptable Use Policy," is an Acceptable Usage Policy (AUP) for an organization with more than 250 users. At the time I worked for them, they had opened their fourth office in the United States and were in negotiations to open an office in Europe. They ran mainframes, UNIX servers, and PCs on the desktop. All the offices were tied together using private lines. This organization wanted something that resembled a summary of their information security policies so that users would have few questions as to the nature of their policies.

The second sample, "Sample Email Security Policy," has to do with email policy. This organization was worried about the spread of email viruses and had just purchased a system that would scan email attachments for viruses. Because this organization hired a lot of young people, management felt that they needed a statement that users would notice on email etiquette. They felt the *Ten Commandments of Email* (see Chapter 7, "Email Security Policies") was the way to communicate their intent. It was their decision to place it at the end of the Email Policy document.

Finally, "Sample Administrative Policies," is a section on administrative policies outlining compliance and enforcement (see Chapter 12, "Compliance and Enforcement"). This sample was adapted from a growing organization that was going through the process of getting ready for their Initial Public Offering (IPO). What makes this sample interesting is the style. Just before we finished all the policies, one of the executives had added a brief explanation, in relatively plain language, of each policy statement and included them within the document. It was called the "Purpose Statement." After a lot of discussion, mostly positive, these statements were left in the documents. However, a disclaimer was added to the introduction of the policies. Although this is the only time I have used this, I would consider using it again under the right circumstances.

Sample Acceptable Use Policy

This document sets forth the policy of _____ (the Company) with regard to the use of, access to, review, and disclosure of various electronic communications, including those sent or received by Company employees. This information systems policy applies to all individuals using the Company's computer and network systems, including employees, subcontractors, and consultants.

For the purposes of this document, "electronic communications" includes, but is not limited to, the sending, receipt, and use of information through the corporate electronic information network, the Internet, voicemail, facsimiles, teleconferencing, and all other online information services.

Information Systems Are for Business Purposes

Information systems offered by the Company are provided to its users for the primary purpose of Company-related use.

Personal use is permissible on a limited basis. This limited personal use should not be during charged time and should not interfere with job performance. Personal messages may not be broadcast to groups of people or other employees except to appropriate forums (such as designated Usenet news groups). Permission for Company-wide broadcasting of personal messages must be obtained from your manager.

Monitoring and Privacy

Electronic communications through the Company's information systems are the property of the Company to assist it in carrying out business. The Company treats all electronic communications sent, received, or stored as business messages, including those for personal use. All users shall have no expectations of privacy with respect to any electronic message. While the Company will not do this routinely, it reserves the right to monitor, access, review, copy, store, or delete any electronic communications, including personal messages, from the system for any purpose and to disclose them to others, as deemed appropriate.

Data Retention Policy

The Company will retain email messages and any backup of such email for six months. Other computer system backups will be stored for only one year or longer if required by contract.

Prohibited Activity and Use of Good Judgment

Use of electronic communications to engage in any communication or action that is threatening, discriminatory (based on language that can be viewed as harassing others based on race, creed, color, age, sex, physical, handicap, sexual orientation, or otherwise), defamatory slanderous, obscene, or harassing is prohibited. Electronic communications shall not disclose personnel information without authorization. The destruction or alteration of electronic communications with the intent to cause harm or injury to the Company or an employee of the Company is strictly prohibited.

Electronic communications shall not be used for any illegal purposes or violate the intellectual property rights of others. Employees shall not break into the computers or intercept the communications of other individuals.

Employees will use the same good judgment to prepare electronic communications as they would use in preparing a hard copy of a memorandum. The content of electronic communications may have significant business and financial consequences for individuals of the Company and may be inappropriately taken out of context. Because of the ease of sending these documents, extra care must be taken to ensure that they are not sent hastily. Please keep in mind that your messages may be read by someone other than the addressee. Accordingly, please ensure that your messages are courteous, professional, and business-like.

Intellectual Property and Licensing

The ease of copying through various electronic communications systems poses a serious risk of intellectual property infringement. Each user must be aware and respect the rights of others.

Software that may be marked as "free," "public domain," and "public use" may be free for personal use but not corporate use. In downloading software from the Internet, use of this software can violate copyright or licensing requirements. Always obtain approval from your manager or the Legal Department before using any publicly available software package.

Do not copy software licensed to the Company unless you are authorized under the Company's license to do so.

Users may not install software that originally came from your home computer or elsewhere unless you can demonstrate from a written license that such use is permitted.

Do not copy software owned by the company without appropriate permissions.

Do not remove intellectual property notices of others.

Virus Protection

Users may not knowingly create, execute, forward, or introduce any computer code designed to self-replicate, damage, or otherwise impede the performance of any computer's memory, storage, operating system, or software.

Software and other files may not be loaded on the Company's computers unless a virus check is performed using an approved virus-scanning program. It is a violation of this policy to disable any virus-checking facilities installed on any system or network.

Disciplinary Action

Management reserves the right to revoke any user's access privileges at any time for violations of this policy and conduct that disrupts the normal operation of the company's information systems. Any conduct that adversely affects the ability of others to use the company's systems and networks or which can harm or offend others, will not be permitted. Violations to this policy can result in termination.

Authority may be exercised without notice, and management disclaims responsibility for loss or damage to data and software as a result.

Acknowledgment

I acknowledge that I have read and will abide by the Company's Information Security Policy.

Sample Email Security Policy

This section sets forth the Company's policy on the use of electronic mail (email) for electronic communications.

Administering Email

The Company is responsible for creating and managing an infrastructure that can support the safe and successful delivery of email within the Company and to customers, partners, and others via the Internet.

As part of this architecture, the Company will create means by which it can scan the content of messages to prevent the spread of viruses, worms, Trojan Horses, or other executable items that could pose a threat to the security of the systems and network.

Email Virus Protection

Email that has been found to be infected with a virus, worm, Trojan Horse, or contains another executable item that could pose a threat to security will not be delivered to the user. Infected email should be removed from the delivery system and analyzed by network and security administrators. Network and security administrators are responsible for creating and maintaining the procedures for handling infected email messages that are consistent with these policies.

Archiving Email

All email is retained and archived. The archive will reside on a server controlled and managed by network and security administrators with access limited to security management, human resource management, and the Company's executive management. This archive may be reviewed at any time so ensure that users are complying with all Company policies. Executive and security management will create a plan for doing this review and outline appropriate remedies for violators.

The email archive will remain online for six months before moved to an offline storage medium. The offline storage will be maintained for two years or longer if required by contract or court order. After two years, the offline medium will be erased or destroyed in a manner commensurate with its technology.

User Responsibilities

Email is the electronic equivalent of a postcard. Anyone can read its contents along the delivery path. Sensitive, confidential, or proprietary information may be sent to users who have access to the local area network. Appropriate information may be sent to customers and partners with connections to the local area network. No sensitive, confidential, or proprietary information may be sent to anyone via the Internet.

All users of the Company's email service will follow and respect the *Ten Commandments of Email:*[1]

1. Thou shalt demonstrate the same respect thy gives to verbal communications.

2. Thou shalt check thy spelling, thy grammar, and read thine own message thrice before thou send it.

3. Thou shalt not forward any chain letter.

4. Thou shalt not transmit unsolicited mass email (spam) unto anyone.

5. Thou shalt not send messages that are hateful, harassing, or threatening unto fellow users.

6. Thou shalt not send any message that supports illegal or unethical activities.

7. Thou shalt remember thine email is the electronic equivalent of a postcard and shalt not be used to transmit sensitive information.

8. Thou shalt not use thine email broadcasting facilities except for making appropriate announcements.

9. Thou shalt keep thy personal email use to a minimum.

10. Thou shalt keep thy policies and procedures sacred and help administrators protect them from abusers.

---

1. These commandments are loosely based on "The Ten Commandments of E-mail Etiquette" attributed to Patricia McIntosh (`fyrewede@concentric.net`), which was sent to many mailing lists (date unknown).

Sample Administrative Policies

PURPOSE: *To establish the policies to administer and enforce these information security policies.*

User Training

PURPOSE: *To ensure all users know and understand the policies.*

POLICY: All users of the Company's networks and systems shall undergo security awareness training to explain these security policies prior to being allowed access. Current users shall undergo training within 30 days from when these policies will be put into effect.

Publishing and Notification

PURPOSE: *To publish the policies to be accessible to all users and to notify them when they are published.*

POLICY: The Human Resources Department shall be responsible for publishing the Information Security Policies and all updates on the Company's intranet. The Human Resources Department shall notify every user that the policies have been published and how they may be accessed.

PURPOSE: *To provide printed copies for those who cannot access the electronic version.*

POLICY: The Human Resources Department shall provide each department and users without access to the intranet one printed copy of these policies at the same time the electronic version is published.

Management Responsibilities

PURPOSE: *To establish the right to monitor.*

POLICY: Management shall monitor all systems activity and network traffic to enforce the provisions of these policies. Management shall be allowed to assign monitoring and other information security duties to appropriate administrators.

PURPOSE: *To establish the right to install access controls.*

POLICY: Management shall install access controls consistent with the requirements of these policies.

PURPOSE: *To establish the right to test the controls.*

POLICY: Management and assigned administrators shall have the responsibility of testing access controls and the network for vulnerabilities. Users shall not test for vulnerabilities and access controls by manual or programmatic means.

PURPOSE: *To warn against exploiting vulnerabilities.*

POLICY: When vulnerabilities are known, users shall not exploit their effects by manual or programmatic means.

PURPOSE: *To limit the use of security and testing tools to management and administrators.*

POLICY: Management and assigned administrators shall have access to the tools that can help manage and test information security. Users shall not have access to these tools on the Company's network. Users shall not load or download these tools from any location.

Administrators' Responsibility

PURPOSE: *To mandate that administrators keep sufficient records of security violations.*

POLICY: Security, systems, and network administrators shall maintain records of all security violations. These records shall be in sufficient detail so that they may be used for disciplinary actions and policy review.

PURPOSE: *To mandate the use of Risk Acceptance Memos as a mechanism to grant waivers to these policies.*

POLICY: Security administrators shall maintain Risk Acceptance Memos for each waiver granted to these policies. Managers who want to ignore a part of these policies must sign that memo accepting responsibility for the security of those systems and networks.

PURPOSE: *To mandate that only systems and network administrators can create and maintain user identification and access control information.*

POLICY: Systems and network administrators shall be designated as the maintainers of user and access control information. These duties shall include the creation and modification of user accounts and changing access controls when necessary.

PURPOSE: *To mandate a semi-annual audit of identification and access controls.*

POLICY: Security, systems, and network administrators shall perform a semi-annual audit of user accounts and associated access controls to ensure validity and accuracy.

PURPOSE: *To mandate administrators define the logging of appropriate systems and network activities.*

POLICY: Security, network, and systems administrators shall define the information that will be saved in systems and network logs. These definitions shall include a record of all security relevant activities.

PURPOSE: *To mandate the review of the various logs and that only designated administrators should be the ones to review them.*

POLICY: Authorized administrators shall review the system and other logs on a regular basis.

PURPOSE: *To mandate the protection of the various logs.*

POLICY: Administrators shall take appropriate precautions to prevent logs from being deactivated, modified, or deleted.

PURPOSE: *To ensure administrators report security violations appropriately.*

POLICY: Administrators shall follow appropriate procedures when discovering violations of these policies or network security.

PURPOSE: *To mandate the backup and archiving of the log files.*

POLICY: Administrators shall back up active logs to an online storage facility. The online backup shall be archived to an offline storage medium on the last day of each month. The offline storage of logs shall be maintained for two years unless contract or the law requires longer periods.

Enforcement and Incident Reporting

PURPOSE: *To establish that everyone is responsible for enforcing these policies.*

POLICY: All users shall be responsible for maintaining and enforcing the provisions of these policies and associated procedures. Violations to these policies and associated procedures shall be reported using the designated reporting procedures.

PURPOSE: *To establish a program of monitoring the various lists that disclose security incidents and software bugs.*

POLICY: Administrators shall monitor public disclosure organizations that report incidents, bugs, and other problems that could affect the security of the Company's network and systems. These public disclosure organizations shall include the vendors of the information systems in use by the Company, at least two general organizations, and the vendor of the Company's chosen anti-virus software.

PURPOSE: *To establish procedures on working with law enforcement.*

POLICY: The response of violations from law enforcement shall be coordinated with management. Management shall be the lead internal investigator and shall take responsibility for interfacing and cooperating with law enforcement.

PURPOSE: *To amplify the requirement to properly handle evidence of security violations.*

POLICY: Data regarding information security violations and incident handling shall be retained so that it may be used during the analysis of the information security policies.

Termination Policy

PURPOSE: *To establish a procedure when a user is voluntarily or involuntarily terminated.*

POLICY: Users whose association with the Company is terminated shall have their access privileges to the Company's resources immediately revoked. Administrators shall arrange for the programs and other data used by these users to be archived. Administrators shall create procedures for revoking access of these users.

Remedies

PURPOSE: *To establish the premise for basic behaviors while using the Company's network and systems.*

POLICY: Any conduct which adversely affects the ability of others to use the company's systems and networks, or which can harm or offend others, shall not be permitted.

PURPOSE: *To establish the right of management to revoke systems and network access to those who violate these policies.*

POLICY: Management shall have the right to revoke any user's access privileges and terminate his or her association with the Company at any time for violations of this policy or demonstration of conduct that disrupts the normal operation of the Company's network and computing systems.

PURPOSE: *To establish the right of management to break agreements and contract with those given access to the systems and network that violate these policies.*

POLICY: Management shall have the right to sever contracts and agreements with contractors and other outside users if they violate this policy or demonstrate conduct that disrupts the normal operation of the Company's network and computing systems.

PURPOSE: *To establish the right of management to report illegal violations to appropriate law enforcement entities.*

POLICY: Management shall have the right to exercise their options under the appropriate criminal and civil laws to seek legal remedies from anyone who uses, abuses, or attacks the Company's network and information systems in a manner that would be in violation of the law and these policies.

Index

A

filtering firewalls, 81

FIPS (Federal Information Processing Standards), 120

firewalls
Internet security policies, 78–81
types of, 81

forensic accounting, 34

G-H

gateways (network security policies), 60

government contracts, developing information security policies for, 6

guest usernames (network security policies), 62–63

hacker organizations, web sites for information, 189

handling data. *See* data handling

hardware, protected by information security policies, 12

HIPAA (Health Insurance Portability and Accountability Act), 132
web sites for information, 189–190

human resources
physical security policies, 50
protected by information security policies, 13

I

ICMP (Internet Control Message Protocol), Internet security policies, 83

illegal activities (compliance and enforcement policies), 160

incident reporting
compliance and enforcement policies, 162–164
auditing policies, 164-165
required actions, 164
sample policy, 201

incident response
planning information security policies, 22-23
computer crime, 23
web sites for information, 185–186

incoming traffic management (Internet security policies), 78–80

industrial espionage, 45

information ownership, 28–30

Information Security Department responsibilities, 31
outsourcing, 32

Information Security Management Committee, 28

information security policies, 3
data security issues, 15
archival storage, 19-20
backup data, 18-19
data disposal, 20
data handling, 15-16
personal and personnel data, 16-17
software licensing, 17-18
defining access, 14
how to develop, 6
approval process, 9
enforcement, 9
number of policies to write, 7
review process, 8
risk assessment, 8
importance of, 4
incident response issues, 22-23
intellectual property rights issues, 20-21
language used, 43
management support for, 4
policies versus procedures, 3-4
review process, 169
information to include, 171-172
review committee, 172
timetable for reviews, 169-171
sample policies, 193-194
administrative policies, 199-202
AUP (Acceptable Use Policy), 195-196
email security policy, 197-198
web sites for information, 191-192

Q-R

T

VOICES THAT MATTER

VISIT OUR WEB SITE

WWW.NEWRIDERS.COM

On our web site, you'll find information about our other books, authors, tables of contents, and book errata. You will also find information about book registration and how to purchase our books, both domestically and internationally.

EMAIL US

Contact us at: **nrfeedback@newriders.com**

- If you have comments or questions about this book
- To report errors that you have found in this book
- If you have a book proposal to submit or are interested in writing for New Riders
- If you are an expert in a computer topic or technology and are interested in being a technical editor who reviews manuscripts for technical accuracy

Contact us at: **nreducation@newriders.com**

- If you are an instructor from an educational institution who wants to preview New Riders books for classroom use. Email should include your name, title, school, department, address, phone number, office days/hours, text in use, and enrollment, along with your request for desk/examination copies and/or additional information.

Contact us at: **nrmedia@newriders.com**

- If you are a member of the media who is interested in reviewing copies of New Riders books. Send your name, mailing address, and email address, along with the name of the publication or web site you work for.

BULK PURCHASES/CORPORATE SALES

If you are interested in buying 10 or more copies of a title or want to set up an account for your company to purchase directly from the publisher at a substantial discount, contact us at 800-382-3419 or email your contact information to corpsales@pearsontechgroup.com. A sales representative will contact you with more information.

WRITE TO US

New Riders Publishing
201 W. 103rd St.
Indianapolis, IN 46290-1097

CALL/FAX US

Toll-free (800) 571-5840
If outside U.S. (317) 581-3500
Ask for New Riders
FAX: (317) 581-4663

RELATED NEW RIDERS TITLES

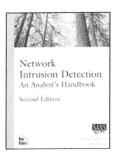

ISBN: 0735710082
480 pages
US$45.00

Network Intrusion Detection: An Analyst's Handbook, Second Edition

Stephen Northcutt and Judy Novak

"This is a great book for anyone interested in learning about how networks really work. It explains how to analyze network traffic, how to identify possible attacks, and how to deal with them. It is the best book I have seen on this subject. The treatment of denial of service attacks is particularly good."

—An online reviewer

ISBN: 0735710635
448 pages
US$39.99

Intrusion Signatures and Analysis

Stephen Northcutt, Matt Fearnow, Karen Frederick, and Mark Cooper

"The real-world signatures in this book, along with the analysis, make this a wonderful reference book. There is, of course, no substitute for experience. However, this book provides an excellent baseline of experience for any intrusion analyst! From that baseline, one should be able to better analyze future attacks."

—An online reviewer

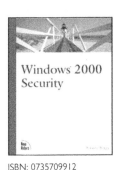

ISBN: 0735710090
800 pages
US$45.00

Hackers Beware

Eric Cole

This book helps readers understand what security threats they are up against and what they need to do to protect against them. Covering the complete picture, it not only describes how a hacking exploit works but presents the signature of the attack, what to look for on a network, and how to protect against it.

ISBN: 0735710996
600 pages
US$44.99

Linux Firewalls, Second Edition

Robert Ziegler

"I've spent countless hours digging through other Linux security books trying to find firewall setup information (particularly ipchains configuration info). This book is far and away the best one I've come across. It felt like it was written specifically for me... I read about half of it in one sitting and was immediately able to debug my firewall setup afterwards."

—An online reviewer

ISBN: 0735709912
575 pages
US$39.99

Windows 2000 Security

Roberta Bragg

"Roberta Bragg is one of the foremost experts on security. I got this book based on her reputation and was not disappointed. Security has a lot of dark passages that can lose you, but this book, since it is dedicated to Win2K, covers all topics in a clear, concise format. It is good for security novices and experts. I have used it to not only understand principles but to gather reference information. An excellent book!"

—An online reviewer

ISBN: 1578702569
400 pages
US$39.99

Incident Response

Eugene Schultz and Russell Shumway

This book provides a comprehensive approach, covering everything necessary to effectively deal with all phases of incident response—spanning from pre-incident conditions and considerations to what takes place at the end of an incident.

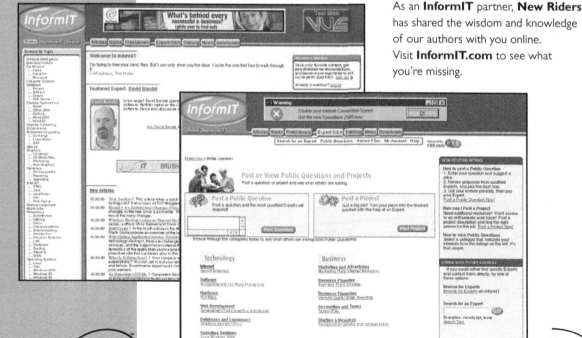

Publishing the Voices that Matter

| web development | graphics & design | server technology | certification |

You already know that New Riders brings you the Voices that Matter.

But what does that mean? It means that New Riders brings you the

Voices that challenge your assumptions, take your talents to the

next level, or simply help you better understand the complex technical

world we're all navigating.

Visit **www.newriders.com** to find:

- ▶ Never before published chapters
- ▶ Sample chapters and excerpts
- ▶ Author bios
- ▶ Contests
- ▶ Up-to-date industry event information
- ▶ Book reviews
- ▶ Special offers
- ▶ Info on how to join our User Group program
- ▶ Inspirational galleries where you can submit your own masterpieces
- ▶ Ways to have your Voice heard

New Riders

WWW.NEWRIDERS.COM

Colophon

The image on the cover of this book, captured by photographer Spike Mafford, is that of an old-growth cedar on Vancouver Island in British Columbia, Canada. Old-growth forests are generally at least 300 years old. Few trees in the world display the size, stature, and life span of these forests. Old-growth forests flourish because they are for the most part undisturbed (by fire, for example, or harvesting).

This book was written and edited in Microsoft Word, and laid out in QuarkXPress. The fonts used for the body text are Bembo and MCPdigital. It was printed on 50# Husky Offset Smooth paper at VonHoffmann Graphics Inc. in Owensville, MO. Prepress consisted of PostScript computer-to-plate technology (filmless process). The cover was printed at Moore Langen Printing in Terre Haute, Indiana, on 12pt, coated on one side.

Visit the Web Site for
Writing Information Security Policies

This site was developed by Scott Barman and includes the following:

- Electronic version of the table of contents in outline format; this can be used to create an initial outline to begin discussions of your organization's security policies

- Full text of Chapter 7, "Email Security Policies"

- Information security links from Appendix B, "Resources," with active HTML links that will be updated and added to as new information on the web becomes available

- Full text of the three sample policies included in Appendix C, "Sample Policies"

- Any updates and corrections that might be necessary

- Updated resources and pointers to articles about writing security policies

Visit the web site at

```
http://www.barman.ws/wisp
```

or

```
http://www.newriders.com
```

www.barman.ws/wisp

www.newriders.com

Made in the USA
Monee, IL
12 February 2022

91091781R00136